FOLLOWING AFTER GOD

Life's Greatest Adventure

MARK SCRIVENER

Parsons Publishing House
Melbourne, Florida USA

FOLLOWING AFTER GOD—Life's Greatest Adventure
by Mark Scrivener

Parsons Publishing House
P. O. Box 410063
Melbourne, FL 32941 USA
www.ParsonsPublishingHouse.com
Info@ParsonsPublishingHouse.com

All Scripture quotations, unless otherwise indicated, are taken from the *Holy Bible, King James Version* (Public Domain).

ISBN -13: 978-1-60273-142-4
ISBN -10: 1-60273-142-x
Library of Congress Control Number: 2022938022

Printed in the United States of America.
For World-Wide Distribution.

Cover Photo by Alma Ward Scrivener.

WHAT PEOPLE ARE SAYING

Dr. Mark Scrivener has brought his life story to the pages of ***Following After God.*** It's an amazing story that weaves its way through meaningful experiences that have shaped the man we know today. His insights, divine encounters, and significant moments with God knit together his faith, hope, encouragement, and wisdom for those who read. Take this journey with Dr. Mark and share the rich experiences that will mark your journey of destiny.—**Dr. Gerald Doggett**, Bishop and Founder, Doggett Leadership Institute, Orlando, Florida USA.

I am glad to call this long, tall Texan a friend. I've found his life defies stereotyping. It's a poem being written, a dream come true from impossible beginnings. Follow Mark through this path of revelations erupting out of yet more impossibilities. The supernatural thing about Mark is his listening ear, finely tuned to the Master's inimitable voice. The actions penned in this book prove it. Your life is a story, too. Come and see how God does this. Mark will be a wonderful tour guide for you.—**Rev. David Christian**, David Christian Ministries, Grandville, Michigan USA, Ecuador and Mexico.

Mark Scrivener is a gifted expositor and teacher of the Word of God. He speaks and writes with clarity, simplicity, and accuracy. May these experiences be a source of encouragement to you in your study of God's Word.—**Randy Bach**, Pastor of Gateway Church, Tacoma, Washington USA.

This book is more than Mark Scrivener's testimony; it is a living example of one man seeking to hear the voice of God and to do His will on earth as it is in heaven.—**Richard Thornhill**, Words of Life Church, Allen, Texas USA.

Be encouraged as you read about one man's walk with the Holy Spirit. Mark has remained full of faith through the trials and victories that we all encounter in life.—**Bruce McQuigg**, Founding Pastor of New Beginnings Church, Hoopeston, Illinois USA.

I met Mark over 30 years ago and realized how powerfully God had moved in his life to call him into the ministry. His testimony of the many supernatural manifestations of God that have continued to accompany his unique journey still leaves me completely fascinated as I read them. Don't be surprised if you pick up this book and can't put it down! This writing should have a sequel already in the works, as God continues to show himself in Mark's experiences. Plus, you will find that Mark's anointed writings spill right over into your own experiences. Thank you, Mark, for sharing your special walk with God to bless his people.—**Benny Thomas**, Benny Thomas Ministries, Beaumont, Texas.

Seventeen years ago, the Lord drew Mark to assist in a new youth endeavor in our Oregon community to help troubled teens. The project laid a foundation for ministry. Over the years, our friendship has come to be something I truly treasure. Since those first days, we have gone on to partner in multiple mission trips and have seen the Lord work in truly remarkable ways. The truth is, everyone has a past, and God can use it if we can learn to trust Him. Mark's life story is another example of how God can take all the broken pieces of our lives and create the most amazing works of art.—**Rick Worlitz**, Senior Pastor of Yankton Community Fellowship, St. Helens, Oregon USA.

With the sole purpose of giving thanks to the Lord Jesus, for having allowed us to know an angel of God, Dr. Mark Scrivener: a Pastor, Evangelist, Missionary, lover of the work of God in Mexico, Central and South America, and someone who helps support works in Africa by taking the gospel to those who need love and the words of hope. Thank God for this angel of God who has shown us the way to salvation with the promise of protection and security in Christ (translated from Spanish).—**Dr. Gilberto Chavez B., M.D.**, Pastor and Director of City of God Orphanage, Jimenez, Coahuila, Mexico.

Dr. Mark Scrivener loves God and people strongly and is willing to do whatever is necessary to follow His lead and bless His children as a humble servant. No doubt, his book will be an inspiration to all who will take the time to walk through its lines! —**Pablo E. Masson**, former pastor at Agape Christian Church, Lima, Perú.

DEDICATION

I dedicate this book to the Lord Jesus Christ of Nazareth, Who loved me and washed me from my sins in His own blood, Who never failed, Who stood with me throughout life, and Who will lead me into death.

I also acknowledge all the dearly departed ones from a country long past: my family of cowboys and Indians—Jews and gentiles, and all who contributed to my life and my salvation.

ACKNOWLEDGEMENTS

I want to give a special thanks to my wife, Alma Ward Scrivener, who is a constant source of support, encouragement, and counsel to me, without whom I could have never put these thoughts into writing.

I want to acknowledge my son, Jason Scrivener, who was sent by God to change me. As I have said many times, *"Jason, someday I will be standing just inside a gate of pearl, looking down an astral highway toward the Earth, waiting to see your precious face among the crowd of travelers. I have always loved you, and I'll be there waiting for you!"*

I want to acknowledge my mentors: the faithful men and women, whom, if I were to mention each by name, I would have to write another book. Some wrote recommendations, one wrote a foreword, some are mentioned in the book and are in heaven, and some are standing with me today, each one focusing my attention on the Lord Jesus Christ and urging me onward. Thank you so much for the hours, days, weeks, months, and years we shared and all you did for me!

Many thanks, also, to Darrell and Diane Parsons, whose help made this book possible.

TABLE OF CONTENTS

FOREWORD

Some folks are like an old shoe, they just fit—comfortable, natural.

Mark was an eager student at Lakewood Bible Institute in Houston. He was not content to just be a Christian in some church as a pew warmer. He wanted more and was willing to commit to the process of maturing in the walk of faith.

We did not get to fellowship much during the classes at Lakewood but during the years following we found opportunities to encourage each other in the faith. He still wants more. His desire is to follow the leading of the Holy Spirit and serve the Body of Christ wherever he goes. You will enjoy reading of the many events and various ways God has worked through Mark to glorify His name.

Mark is not one to "shout it from the housetops" when God uses him in the supernatural, but it is a natural flow of events. Oftentimes, he had to look back to recognize the hand of God because there were no "Holy Ghost goosebumps" or any physical manifestations. He is an excellent demonstration of how God often moves supernaturally in the natural.

Mark's word is good. He is straightforward and honest in his relationships with people. "What you see is what you get" with Mark. No pretense.

This book is Mark's story of his learning to be obedient to the voice of God, to hear and to respond in obedience. A noble ambition for all of us. But it is more than his testimony, it is a living example of one man seeking to hear the voice of God and to do His will on earth as it is in heaven.

May God bless you in the reading of Mark's book that you may see His hand working in your life. He has been there all the time. His plans for you are peace and well-being. He has an eternity planned for all those who will trust Him.

Richard Thornhill
Pastor, Words of Life
Former Professor, Lakewood Bible Institute
Allen, Texas USA

INTRODUCTION:

The Importance of Testimony

I was very thankful for that attic fan! Being inside with no breeze would have made the summer nights unbearable in southeast Texas in those days before air conditioning. As I lay in bed watching the moonlight, the fan produced a white drone, and the suction would make the curtains dance in the wind coming through the open windows. Even though the nighttime temperatures could exceed 80 degrees, the 90% humidity caused a cooling effect that was actually comfortable after a few minutes. At five years of age, the fear of the unknown and the things lurking under the bed made the night a scary place, but the comfort of knowing that my daddy was just in the next room made the monsters hide. That night in 1960, like so many others of my childhood, has been indelibly imprinted on my heart.

Very near that place in my mind and my heart, right next to memories of those hot and dusty roads of my East

Texas youth, dwells the memory of this comforting presence that extended past what I felt from my father. I look back now and realize the sweet air of the Holy Spirit has always been there. Even before I knew God, His Spirit brought me peace in the turmoil and comfort in the drama of life.

It may seem amusing, but it was a great surprise to learn that many people don't view the supernatural as normal because my life has always been naturally supernatural. It seems that someone would follow me and appear from time to time in my dreams or in the night at an area very close to the imagination. When I least expected it, as I closed my eyes, a fleeting image would hurtle past my field of view and seemed to occur on the inside of my eyelids with a subtlety that made it hard to glimpse.

Those memories from my childhood represent a time when things were simple and included an air of majesty. The colors were brilliant, and the smells touched a place inside that insisted there was a grand epic stitched into the very fabric of my life ahead.

This is the beginning of my story and the beginning of my testimony. Now that I am older, I am called a nighttime person by many, and they are correct. The monsters under my bed are gone, and now the nighttime is a wonderful world where I can truly see in the darkness. The noise of the daytime does not clutter the experiences of twilight. It is my favorite time and place. Since my time as a young boy, the ever-faithful Holy Spirit has been my greatest ally in life, and the relationship He has worked so hard to develop with me has become my greatest treasure.

From Memories to Testimony

"And they overcame him by the blood of the Lamb, and by the word of their testimony; and they loved not their lives unto the death" (Revelation 12:11).

Our memories are the basic building blocks of testimony. For the obedient Christian, those memories exist in a spiritual realm where God lives in a form that is as tangible as a present-day reality. The telling of our stories is the testimony drawn from our memories, which is the seed upon which we build many tomorrows. Christian victory, and the testimony of that victory, is empowered by the supernatural action of God's Word carefully woven by the hand of the Master Tailor and activated by our faith through obedience to it. Victory comes from God, and the testimony of those victories overcomes the devil because God is omnipresently active in telling that memory. The undeniable proof of a personal and living testimony should accompany all true teaching of the Word of God; otherwise, it is unproven. While the Bible contains the seed of life in itself, without the personal testimony of the obedient preacher, it can only be a parroted message and dryly religious.

God is the Word Being, and that is why telling our testimonies is so important. Even though the word of our testimony speaks of the past, God lives through it in the here and now. Through that testimony, faith is birthed in the hearts of the hearers, and Jehovah walks out of the past across the bridge of faith and causes someone's present to change forever.

God is much different than what we have become. The world, in its fallen state, is opposed to God's normal. Our everyday normal is a horrible corruption in comparison to what He planned and created. Many old books written about Jewish history and legend insinuate that in their original form, Adam and Eve would be unrecognizable to us today, as would their unfallen world. Our Earth is a rebel colony that exists in the middle of God's World. To man, God's World seems exotic and alien. However, if we choose to cross over through the portal opened to us by the testimony of the apostles, we will stand with them at the foot of the cross and peer into the empty tomb. In that instant, Jesus of Nazareth will walk through the closed doors of our hearts, at which time we will access the living, breathing Lord who conquered death, hell, and the grave. Then down the road that leads to God's World, we shall go.

God's World is like a cord, wrapped around and through us, weaving in and out of what we call reality. It is just beyond our field of view and is what remains after all is said and done. Everything grafted by faith into that World becomes eternal in us. To Jesus, the Lord of all worlds and His reality, we will learn to conform. One job of the Holy Spirit is to teach us to align and accustom ourselves to that World while we live our lives here on Earth. As we do, we become more at home in the spirit, and we begin to see the Word work in our natural lives, making us more like Jesus. As we voluntarily conform to the teaching of God's Spirit, we encounter that irresistible force that encases us, causing this world to become of less consequence except for the souls of men.

Testimony! As we walk with Jesus, He manifests Himself in our natural world. The Living God, who walks and talks with us, shows up when we least expect Him and in the strangest ways. Therefore, when building a testimony, we should well-remember what the Bible says in Matthew 24:44, "Therefore be ye also ready; for in such an hour as ye think not the Son of man cometh." When Jesus appears in our lives, usually it is when we are not expecting Him, so we must watch and be alert!

My Testimony

In the ministry, I have served in many places, doing many things for the Lord Jesus. In 1992, I was a missionary living at the corner of Calle Grimaldo del Solar and Calle Schell in Lima, Peru, in an apartment on the 8*th* floor of a building. It is my custom to pray in the Holy Ghost as much as possible. Praying in tongues taps us into God's World and connects us to His reality, which can bleed over into our ordinary lives in a manner much greater than what we experience without that type of power-prayer. On that particular day, I had prayed for four hours. Immediately afterward, I was walking down the hall in the apartment, minding my own business, and with no warning, I was suddenly in the spirit; it was as if I was knocked to the floor. I was lying on my back, and an invisible someone pried my mouth open, and in 3-dimensional technicolor, a giant #2 pencil appeared, and the invisible someone began to force it down my throat. I remember how uncomfortable the whole ordeal was, but it was over as fast as it began. Still in the vision, I said, *"Lord! What was that?"* He said, *"That is the anointing to write."* Then I was on my feet in the hall, and I continued on my way.

The apostle John said it well:

> There are also many other things which Jesus did, the which, if they should be written every one, I suppose that even the world itself could not contain the books that should be written (John 21:25).

If each of us were to write our stories of what Jesus did for us, the world itself couldn't contain the books.

Our testimonies can be so vast that all we can do is share bits and pieces of them. This work represents a tiny part of my story. If we continue to follow Jesus throughout our lives and walk in obedience to His Spirit, our stories can become an extension of His Story; they can be so large that we could never write it all. I trust that I can do Him justice because as you read with open-hearted faith, the God of the testimony, who is no respecter of persons, will walk out of the words, off the page, and into your life. He is that very testimony.

1

MY YOUTH

"There is no saint without a past, no sinner without a future." ~ St. Augustine[1]

In the days before freeways, southeast Texas was an interesting place. Metro-Houston is about the size of the state of Rhode Island, but back then, it was not the five-county megalopolis that it is today. On the west side, the city limits did not extend out as far as what later came to be known as the 610 Loop. As a young child, I remember squirrel hunting in the swampy jungle along the Buffalo Bayou near what is known today as "Uptown" or "the Galleria." Most roads were paved until they came to Post Oak Road, but after that, the roads were dirt, and very few people lived among the farms and ranches that made up western Harris County. I remember the dust that would fill the air from the white oyster shell used to pave the road. Today, while driving along Post Oak Boulevard, through the traffic lights and skyscrapers of Uptown, it is hard to imagine that world of yesterday. However, that was the reality in which I was raised, and it is a place I often visit in my heart with much fondness.

Like many baby boomers, my family was troubled from very early on. From a human standpoint, I never understood my upbringing or my difficulties, many of which resulted from that upbringing. I can relate to something I once heard someone say, *"The Bible says if you spare the rod, you hate your son... well, my mother loved me!"*

I readily admit that I would appreciate having had a more normal childhood. However, when taking account of my life from a purely spiritual standpoint at this late date, I do not regret my upbringing. On the contrary, it helped make me aware of the flaws that exist in my character, which had to be confronted to successfully go forward with Jesus. That hardness also gave me the resilience to face whatever comes against me with courage and enabled me to take my stand alongside the Jewish Messiah. There has to be a certain toughness to walk by faith and not by sight, and my youth gave me that quality.

My maternal grandmother—a Christian woman—was a source of love for me, and I spent many weekends at her home. She was born in Fort Scott, Kansas, descended from the Irish-Cherokee Indians of the Missouri Ozarks. In 1930 she married Papa, a Sephardic Jewish shoemaker recently come from Italy who moved to Texas. There always seemed to be a big pot of "spaghetti red" cooking on the stove, and the smells of her kitchen still waft through my memories. As I went with the men to go squirrel hunting in the old days, I can clearly remember her voice shouting out the backdoor, *"Watch for snakes!"* That sage advice has helped me with all the people who came in and out of my life; my grandmother helped me watch out for snakes—especially the two-legged variety.

My grandmother was more like my mother than my mother was. Mother had her own issues, which were magnified by her drinking. Grandma was a closet Pentecostal but tried to keep peace with my grandpa by never discussing the subject with anyone.

My grandparent's home was a wonderland made for exploration, filled with nooks, crannies, and boxes filled with surprises. As the days went on, I would find myself lying on the floor in front of their fireplace, reading a book, or watching black-and-white television. On the mantle of that fireplace was placed a small and white figurine made of porcelain; it was shaped like praying hands with a book in front of it inscribed with the words, "God Is Love." As soon as I could read, I felt something tug at my heart every time I looked at that figurine.

Around that same time, my parents sporadically attended a little Baptist church on a dirt road in the piney prairies of cattle country to the northwest of Houston. The pastor was a good man who loved his congregation; his message was one of hellfire and brimstone, with the grace of the cross mixed in. With great difficulty, I would strain to see over the pew in front of me. I vividly remember sitting with a crayon and a hymn book and feeling the tap on my shoulder and the concerned look on the face of the man in the pew behind us as he reminded me not to use my crayon to decorate the hymn book!

On Easter Sunday when I was seven years old, the pastor preached, and in his sermon, he said:

> *"I had a dream. In my dream, I saw a long-haired man who was chained to a wall, naked from the waist up, and there was a Roman soldier with his back to me with a horrible whip-like scourge. He was beating the man. During the beating, the chained man turned His head so that I could see His face, and I recognized Him, by the crown of thorns and the anguished look, that He was the Lord Jesus Christ. I was horrified! It seemed as if the soldier would lean back and heave into the whip with all his might and laugh out loud in demonic glee with each stripe as the Lord screamed in pain, while pieces of His back splattered in the blood and gore of the dreaded Roman scourge! In my dream, after a couple of stripes with the whip, I couldn't take it anymore! I thought, 'How could that evil soldier enjoy such a horrible thing so much? I can't let him keep beating my Lord!' At that moment, in my revulsion and outrage, I ran up behind him and forcefully laid my hand on his shoulder and turned him around, and when I saw his face, to my shock, it was me! I was the Roman soldier!"*[2]

Listening to his message, I remember the feeling of what seemed like my heart coming up in my throat; I couldn't hold back the tears. His dream illustrated to me my guilt in the Lord's death and that, in my own way, I had taken part in His crucifixion. Upon understanding that Jesus died on purpose to open a way for me to come to God, when the time came to receive Christ as Savior, at seven years of age, I was the first one to go to the altar. In my heart, I was crying out, "*Jesus Christ, Son of God, have mercy on me: a sinner!*" Looking up at the Pastor through my tears, I remember the compassion in his eyes. He knelt in front of me and whispered in my ear, "*Do you understand what you're doing?*" I said, "*Yes, I do. I want to accept Jesus in my heart.*" He said, "*Are you willing to be baptized?*" I was willing, and the Pastor led me in the prayer of salvation at that moment. I will never forget the euphoria and what felt like dancing on the inside when Jesus came into my heart, and I was born-again. I was overjoyed, and that night, on June 23, 1963, I was baptized in water and began my Christian life.

After that time, my childhood was difficult, complete with the heartache of losing contact with my dear father through my parent's divorce and what seemed like constant physical and emotional whippings. As a result, I was a very troubled child.

My mother remarried in 1964. At that time, in my brokenness, I did not appreciate my mother's new husband; however, in the end, he turned out to be a good and decent man. He had two boys my age and was a hard-drinking United States Air Force Reserve Officer of German descent. He truly loved his family and was a wonderful provider, but he was a hard man. I have often said that I owe my stepfather a debt that I could never repay because his presence kept me away from many things that would have led to my destruction. My life was not less difficult, but I survived!

After my mother's new marriage, if I attended church at all, it was only at Easter or Christmas, and although I had a Bible, I could not understand it. All I could remember from those short few months in church was my salvation experience and a few elementary Sunday School lessons, but I would often pray during my regular times of need. In the fall of 1968, when I was 13, I was plagued by stomachaches triggered by fear surrounding fights at school, problems at home, along with the horror of missing my father, who had moved to Virginia. All of this combined to make me a sad young man.

Despair is a horrible thing. It is a deviation from what God planned for us. Joy and happiness should fill our lives, but many times that is not the case. Sadness is usually rooted in fear and worry, and the sicknesses I suffered in my youth were emotional and associated with worry. My mother took me to the doctor, but no physical illness was found.

Our home was on the west side of old Houston. It was a comfortable three-bedroom, two-bath ranch-style house with my room in the front with the den between it and the kitchen. When I was alone and worried or afraid, I would pace from my room through the den, to the kitchen, and back to my bedroom and pray.

One day, I had a stomachache and stayed home alone from school. I was worried about what was wrong with me and felt a hopelessness that is hard to describe, but in the back of my mind, I could somehow see the figurine on my grandmother's mantle; the words "God Is Love" kept echoing in my heart. As I paced, all I could say was, *"God,*

I need You! Please help me, Jesus!" On that particular day, after about thirty minutes of walking and praying, I passed by the entry hall and felt something gently but forcefully hit me in the head like a piece of sheetrock, but it did not hurt. I stopped in my tracks and looked up, and the ceiling was still there.

As I was absorbed in my thoughts, wondering what that could have been, I noticed at an almost subconscious level that I had begun to mumble in a strange gibberish. I had never successfully read the Bible, nor had I any training in the Pentecostal belief system. I did not know what was going on, and it startled me, so I threw my hand over my mouth and said to myself, "*I must be watching too much Bugs Bunny! I better stop that, or they will think I'm crazy.*" At 13 years of age, nothing in my life felt spiritual. I was so undone that I thought I must have mental problems on top of everything else, and the fear of being found out made me withdraw.

That strange experience did not make my life any easier, but as time went by, that language would show up when I would least expect it, and it seemed to give me a tremendous peace that was so out of place with the rest of my life. As a part-time Baptist, I didn't know anything about speaking in tongues. I found out later that some of my relatives were Pentecostal, but they never spoke of their beliefs around me. It was not until several years later that I understood what had happened to me.

My young teenage years in Texas were a nightmare. I wanted to live with my father but couldn't, so I became an angry teenager and began to rebel by stealing cigarettes, drinking whiskey, and smoking marijuana. Even though my mother and stepfather told me to stay away from the "Holy Rollers"—especially Uncle Wallace, a retired Holy Ghost preacher—I gravitated toward him all the more at that time. I was sent to rehab when I was 16, but when the doctor found I had no addictions, he asked me about my homelife. I thought everyone lived like we did; the doctor's jaw dropped open when he realized my idea of a normal life. At that point, he firmly suggested I go live with my father.

When I was 16, I was finally allowed to go to Virginia Beach to live with my daddy, who was a spiritual man of the Coushatta Indians. It had been nine years since he had lived with us, and when I arrived, I was still an angry kid. Daddy couldn't do much with me, but he tried. I remember going out and getting drunk at a sailor's house. My father tried to sit me down and talk some sense to me. Instead of sitting down, I squared off with him and started cussing. He did the worst thing he could have probably done when he put his face in his hands and cried. I apologized and quit doing those things.

One day around the end of my senior year, I was walking down a mall with a group of kids, and we saw two men in beautiful blue uniforms. I had no idea who they were, but I knew I wanted one of those suits! So, at 17, I joined the United States Marine Corps, and they fixed a bunch of my issues.

After a less than two-year enlistment and an honorable discharge, I decided to try out the hippie lifestyle. I moved to Los Angeles and lived in a park for six months while smoking cigarettes and marijuana and drinking heavily. I learned from the hippies that I did not like being hungry and not having a place to live. So, one day I prayed, *"Lord, I want to go back to Texas, so please help me get a job."* I went to the day labor dock at the Los Angeles Workforce Commission, and after standing there for five minutes, a stranger walked up to me and offered me a job working with trees. My new job enabled me to get a small place to stay, and I saved my money and eventually moved back to East Texas.

"I will never leave thee, nor forsake thee"
(Hebrews 13:5).

Little Ma'am was my great-grandmother on my mother's side. She was a Cherokee Indian maiden—one of eighteen children—from Mountain Grove, Missouri, but raised her family in Ft. Scott, Kansas. After Grandpa Jack died, she began spending six months with family in Kansas City and six months in Texas. Among all my relatives, she seemed to be the one who understood me the most, so I enjoyed listening to her. In her later years, she suffered from cataracts and was blind. From my earliest memories, on New Year's Day, she would say out loud, *"This year, I'll be in Jerusalem!"* When I asked her when she was going to Israel, she explained:

> *"Son, I am not going to Israel; I am going to New Jerusalem in heaven. I love you and don't want to leave you, so I want you to understand my heart. This is not my world or my country, and I'm not at home here. I don't understand your music or your way of*

> *life. All my people are there already, and they're waiting for me. The Lord Jesus is there with my parents. My brothers, sisters, and husband are there with two of my children, along with all my relatives and friends. My heart longs so much to go home."*

I did not really understand what she meant until I turned 60, but what she said stayed with me.

In the spring of 1976, after I returned to Texas in my early 20s, Little Ma'am was 93 and got sick. My grandmother took her to the hospital in Houston. For a week, as her blood pressure dropped, she prayed in tongues rather loudly and kept shouting, *"Jesus is the only Salvation!"* As her mortal life ebbed away, those in the room with her testified about her conversations from the Other Side with people long departed. Finally, on the morning of June 10, 1976, her granddaughter smuggled her infant great-great-grandson into the room to meet her, and later that afternoon, her dream was fulfilled as she finally went to New Jerusalem. It happened as she was deeply involved in a conversation with her husband "Jack," who had passed away in 1948. Grandpa had come, and in the spirit, from her sickbed, she took his hand, got up, and went on an afternoon stroll, walking away together into eternity—finally home!

While she was with us, we would sometimes sit together on the sofa at my grandmother's home, where I would listen to stories of days gone by—a place of covered wagons, horses, Indian tribes, and woodland trails. Little

Ma'am was very sensitive to the Holy Spirit. As we sat when I was older, she would perceive something in the spirit, gently take my hand, and say, *"Little Mark, remember, our people cannot drink alcohol, but Jesus will be with you. So, if you go into certain places and do certain things, even then He walks with you, so try to think about the places and situations where you are taking the Holy Ghost!"* As for me, with God's help, I shudder to say I trust I have learned that lesson.

In those days, the marijuana laws of Texas were quite severe. If arrested, the smallest remains of one marijuana cigarette in the ashtray of the car was a felony that carried a lengthy prison sentence. For about six months, I would buy marijuana from a young man I knew in west Houston. One Friday, as was my custom, I went by his house and pulled into his driveway. Suddenly, with no warning, I heard an audible voice inside the pickup that said, *"Don't go in there!"* I jumped and looked around, expecting to see someone, but no one was there. I was unsure if God was speaking to me because I was certain He would turn me in for that type of behavior. Since I was already nervous because of the staunch prison sentence if caught, I left and planned to return some other time. I went home, and after an hour or so, I called the young man's house to check on him. His wife answered hysterically and said that the Sheriff's Department had kicked down the door with a search warrant and found a pound of marijuana and some barbiturates; my friend had been arrested. I asked her when all of that happened, and she said, *"About an hour ago!"* I was shocked when I realized that was around the time that the voice told me not to go in there! I had never known before what "God is love" really meant; He kept me out of trouble and out of prison. After that, I began telling everyone that Jesus was my Friend, and nobody understood just how big a Friend He was to me.

[1]Briton Hadden and Henry Robinson Luce, Time Incorporated, volume 33 (1939): 21. Quote often attributed to Augustine of Hippo, but this source attributes it to Ahmad Sohráb.

[2]J. W. McDonald, Sunday Sermon, June 23, 1963, Clay Road Baptist Church, Houston , Texas.

2

JESUS SAID HE WANTS TO HEAL YOU

Having God speak to me in different ways seemed normal, but I thought that I must have done something wrong because of the hardness of life during my teenage years. I wondered, *"Did that God, who my grandmother said is 'Love,' abandon me in this situation?"* Suffering can make things appear bleak, and it seemed like those years would never end. Therefore, I desired to get as far away from the pain as I could, so I was drawn to the forests north of Houston where there was a cabin on some land that my grandfather owned. The forest was my friend. It consisted of underbrush, pine, and hardwoods and was so thick that walking through it was nearly impossible unless a trail could be found. The air smelled like perfume, the flowers made everything a blaze of color, and there seemed to be animals everywhere I looked. What I liked most of all was that in those early days, there were no people! It was quiet, and I could be alone!

Today in my messages, I quote a line from an old rock'n'roll song that says, "There's no easy way to be free." When we try to avoid something, that "something" will find us. Pain is an indicator of something wrong, so instead of avoiding our pain, we should confront it, and find out what is broken. Therefore, it is logical to say that we need our pain until it no longer serves a purpose. When we deal with its source through the blood of Jesus, and the pain begins to leave us, it is good to remember what it felt like, lest we should ever forget.

During that time, because of my lifestyle, I was involved in a serious automobile accident. I was in a 1973 Thunderbird that careened off a winding country road in the forest at over 100 MPH. I awakened in a Huntsville, Texas hospital with a separated pelvis, reattached left thumb, broken front teeth, paralysis from the waist down, and horrible pain in my back that never stopped hurting. I cried all day and dreamed of pain at night. A hospital in Houston became my temporary residence. Medical science could do nothing except try to manage the pain with Demerol injections three times a day. My legs were numb, and I was unable to walk. I lived with the humiliation of being carried to the restroom by nurses with the doctors talking about a lifetime of pain management and trying to get me on government assistance. I could not deal with the thought of such a thing at that young age. Of all the things I had to deal with, the worst thing was the thought of how I had ruined my life. I pleaded with God for healing, but I suffered condemnation over what I had done to myself. I thought God would be correct if He did not want to help someone like me. However, God is much better than we thought! His goodness is beyond description, and He reveals it more and more with each passing day! The goodness of God is a progressive revelation.

As the Bible says in Ephesians 2:4, "But God, who is rich in mercy...." I have quoted this verse many times throughout my life since then; it is an active revelation and just keeps getting bigger!

One day, while experiencing great pain in the hospital, the telephone rang. On the line was a Cherokee Uncle, who for many years had been an Evangelist in Kansas, Missouri, and Arkansas, who happened to be in Houston at the time. He sounded very happy and said, *"I heard you're having a hard time!"* I said, *"Yes sir, I sure am."* He said, *"Well, the Lord Jesus said He wants to heal you!"* I said, *"How do you know?"* He laughed and said, *"He spoke to me and said so!"* I said, *"If He wants to do that for me, please tell Him to do it!"* He laughed some more and said, *"OK, it's done then!"* I said, *"Aren't you going to pray?"* He said, *"I already did, and Jesus said that He wants to heal you. It was up to you to agree or disagree, and since you agree, it's done! Let me know what happens,"* and then he hung up.

After the phone call, I didn't feel any different right away. As I lay there, my mind began to wander, thinking of what to make of the conversation, when suddenly I was snapped out of my daydream by the absence of pain! Pain had become a lifestyle, and now it was gone. It can feel strange not to hurt when one has been in pain for that long. Gradually, I noticed a different sensation, like a burning and tingling in my legs, as if the circulation was returning after being cut off, and then suddenly, the pain was gone, and I could feel my legs! I lay very still, thinking that it was a fluke, and if I moved around too much the horrible pain would come back. I was concerned that I might be doubting God the Father, but as I contemplated Him, I could picture a smile as if He were saying, *"It's done! Trust Me!"* After a minute or two, I moved around carefully and felt no pain. I sat up and disconnected all the devices and contraptions and slowly got out of bed. I stood up, walked gingerly around the room, and jumped up and down just to be sure. It was true, and I was so excited!

I wanted to tell everyone, so I went out into the hallway and ran. As I ran by the nurses' station, I told them rather loudly that Jesus had healed me. Strangely, they did not rejoice with me! Instead, they pushed some buttons, made some calls, chased me down, and made me go back into the room, where I began to put on my clothes to leave (I was still feeling the effects of the Demerol but with no pain). While putting on my shirt, the doctor came rushing into the room. He scolded me and told me that I was just adjusting to the pain of the condition and that I needed to get back in bed. I explained what happened and told him that I believed that Jesus had healed me. He did a brief examination. When he saw that the feeling had returned, and he could not initiate a pain response, he said, "*Well, I'll be! I guess you should go home then!*"

Since that time, I have not had a relapse of anything that indicates there was ever a back injury. However, on about ten occasions in the 45 years since then, I have felt a slight twinge of pain in those same areas. It reminds me of what I went through and how kind Jesus has been to me, but I do not play with it, so I stomp my foot and say, *"Oh no, you don't! In Jesus' Name, you get out of here! I am healed by the stripes of the Lord Jesus Christ,"* and it goes away.

Beginning with my healing, day after day, the reality of Jesus continues to surprise me. That experience opened my eyes to a different way of looking at things. God was not the source of my problems! He had not abandoned me. Instead, I discovered that I had been deceived, and it was I who had abandoned God. When I accepted that truth and asked God to forgive me for leaving Him, the process of deliverance began.

3

FAMILIES ARE FOREVER

When I was in the fourth grade, I saw a girl. I noticed that she was different than other people, and the more I considered her and her smile, the stranger things became. I felt some things I had never felt before. I felt a little dizzy, and I was not even sick! It made me curious, so I began to talk to her, and I found out that I *really* liked her! What did it mean to like a girl? What was going on? Why would talking to a girl make my head swim like that?! It was a mystery, but somehow, I knew I wanted to "go around" with her, so I asked her if she would be my girlfriend. I had no idea what all the feelings were about or precisely what a girlfriend was, but I heard birds chirping, saw flowers everywhere, and felt a physical high that can only be described as puppy love. When I got to school, I knew where she would be, and instead of being with my friends, I would hurry to be with her because I knew she would be there waiting and smiling. Even though I was bashful (which was a 1960s word for introverted), I always had something to say. Suddenly at nine years of age, my life had changed, and I had a relationship. Even at that young age, in my heart, it was no longer just me; now, there was another which made me behave differently. That relationship ended a year later, but it taught me some truths.

For Christianity to be genuine, it must be a real interpersonal relationship between the devotee and God, through and in the Name of the living, breathing God-Man, Jesus of Nazareth. Like any relationship, it must bring about a change in lifestyle, and it can only be lived by faith that works and is lived by love.

Many people want to know what it means when we talk about having a relationship with God, and considering any relationship will help us understand it. The way we behave in any good human relationship is the same way we must act in a relationship with God, or our relationship is not real.

We must ask ourselves some questions about our supposed relationship with God: Is there communication? Is there give and take? Does the relationship grow? It may begin being a 50-50 proposition, but it should grow as time goes by and eventually become 100-100 with each person giving his all. Is there a genuine physical and emotional change based on that relationship? Do both parties publicly acknowledge the other?

How would a spouse react to a relationship with no communication or where the other party is stingy with their time and possessions? How would they feel if the other party is ashamed to mention their name in public? Religion can never fulfill the requirements of relationship and meet human needs as only the person of Jesus Christ can.

Karl Marx said, "Religion is the opium of the masses." Mr. Marx was an atheist; his moral and political world view has caused heartache and death on a global scale, but what he said about religion is true. Deep inside, each person has a painful conviction screaming that something is wrong. Much like a hospice where the opiate morphine is used to make a terminal patient more comfortable, what we see in many Christian circles today is a lifeless religion that only serves to deaden that conviction without treating the terminal illness, known as separation from God. Religion does not help anyone; like a drug, it just numbs the pain in the heart that is supposed to be a signpost directing us to Christ.

Religion and going to church will not satisfy the conviction; any more than a shot of morphine will heal cancer. The drug called "religion" is our attempt to satisfy what is missing on the inside without having to change. We can be very religious church members without ever having faced our pain. Our religion can be demonstrated by going to a dead church and allowing it to stay dead. It can be accompanied by social drinking, drugs, meetings or clubs, self-help groups, the occult, sex, or possessions. Instead of trying to avoid it, we must follow that conviction to the cross. Only through the healing balm of the blood of Jesus received at the foot of the cross do we receive answers to our questions and the ability to move beyond ourselves and our selfish ambitions. That relationship with God can empower us to do something that, with time, can actually help people, sometimes on a national or global scale. When we remove the mask of ambition and religion and cast down the foolish explanations of human reasoning, we can honestly perceive the cross, which births a love inside us and changes us from the inside out.

How can we change when we do not know that something is wrong? Somehow, we must be forced to be blatantly honest with ourselves and acknowledge that internal pain. There must be a catalyst to bring about true change, and when that catalyst is a person, object, or goal, it can give us the necessary focus to birth a heartfelt commitment that will cause someone to die a martyr's death for another.

The Christian life is sacrifice, and its enduring symbol is the electric chair of the day: the cross. We must find a reason to die, and then instead of dying, live!

"For there is one God, and one mediator between God and men, the man Christ Jesus" (1 Timothy 2:5). The Bible says that there is only one Man who can mediate between God and man, and He sits on God's Right Hand (Mark 16:19). He is none other than the Lord Jesus Christ. Giving oneself to that Love is the power of Christianity; it is what moved God to become a man forever. Love sent Jesus to the cross and raised Him from the tomb. The commitment moved God, and it must move us, or it is not genuine.

I had met Jesus, and I knew of His Power because I had experienced so much. However, Christianity is more than knowing facts and seeing things. In His wisdom, Jesus saw that I needed a catalyst to be successful in this Christian life: someone I loved more than myself and for whom I could give my life. So, one more time, He delivered me!

On June 3, 1976, I received a telephone call, and someone told me that my son had been born. That was a shock to a 20-year-old! I was totally unprepared for fatherhood, and the only thing I could think to do was call my daddy on the telephone and ask for his advice. I called his number collect from a pay telephone, saying, *"Daddy, I just heard that I became a father!"* He said, *"What is it, a boy or a girl?"* I said, *"It's a boy, but I don't know what to do!"* He said, *"Well, you are going to the hospital, right? When you go, remember that you will enter the room as you are now and come out changed."* It didn't take long for me to understand what he meant. I was still not living right at the time.

Jason entered the world at Jefferson Davis Hospital in Houston. A nurse asked me what I was there for when I arrived, and I said, *"I was told I had a baby today."* She asked my name and returned in a few minutes with a tiny baby boy. She gently pushed him against my chest; I said, *"Wait a minute! How do I know this is the right one?"* She pointed at the nursery and said, *"Baby! How many other white babies do you see up in here?"* I took him in my arms, and immediately when I touched him, God said very clearly in my heart, *"Mark, if you don't change, he's going to hell!"* I was shaken to the core, and in the shaking, my heart broke! I thought that I deserved whatever bad things had happened to me, but I couldn't imagine that innocent baby suffering for my behavior! My father was correct; from the pieces of my broken heart, there flowed a power I had never known before, and it changed me more than anything that had happened since the Baptism in the Holy Spirit! My life was different.

Years later, Jason and I were discussing the subject of his salvation. He was saved at church and received the Baptism of the Holy Spirit with the evidence of speaking in tongues in his sleep when he was four years of age, but when he was 24, he was questioning, like many do.

I knew he was saved because I was there when it happened, but he did not remember a lot of it. I said:

> *"Jason, God made a promise to me on the day you were born. He told me you would go to hell if I didn't change. I changed, and you are going to heaven! Your salvation is between God and me! You are going to do the will of God with your life, whether you do it on your feet or on your knees. He promised me. You are like an inanimate object as far as I'm concerned, and God is going to do His Will in your life."*

Almost twenty years have passed since that conversation, and today Jason is a fine Christian husband and father living in South America. It would help Christian parents to remember that families are forever, and the promises concerning children are made by God to the parents. If the parents continue in faithfulness, God will somehow reach the children; it is a matter of His integrity.

4

SETTING THINGS STRAIGHT

"The water is wide, I can't cross over, and neither have I wings to fly. Build me a boat that can carry two, and both shall row, my love and I."[3]

My grandmother had a friend who was the pastor of a church in Houston. From the time I was discharged from the Marine Corps, he would try to call me on the telephone and invite me to his church. For some odd reason, I always avoided him, but in 1977 I opened the door to Pastor John Osteen. I was invited to Lakewood Church and went on a Wednesday night. I walked in the door, and a greeter hugged my neck, and just like in 1963 at the Baptist church, my heart came up in my throat. So, I started going to church.

I did the best that I could do with my life, trying to make sense of things and do what I had to do to help my son. As much as possible, I tried to keep occupied in Christian activities. One night I was at a home meeting where people were worshiping the Lord. A young lady next to me was praying in the same language that I began to experience when I was 13. I asked her what language she was speaking, and she said she was speaking in other tongues and showed me where it was mentioned in the Bible. I said, *"I've been doing that since 1968!"* She briefly explained it to me, and I began to do it on purpose. Thus, my life with the church began.

The Presence at the Altar

A church can be a strange place. Whether it is a cathedral with 50-foot-high ceilings or a backstreet storefront, one can sense a Presence upon walking in. When I was a child, I naturally thought that Presence was God, Who must surely live there someplace. At first, it seemed only natural to sit toward the back because we are to be humble; I thought, *"Everyone knows that if you are humble, you get as far back as you can!"*

Today, however, when choosing a place to sit in a Holy Ghost meeting, I like to be at the front because the altar and pulpit are the places from where the power flows. Even though God's throne is not a place that can be touched with our fallen senses, it can be found on Earth about two feet on the other side of the pulpit, where the Pastor stands. I am not talking about the lectern; I am talking about that unseen place that exists inside the person standing there under the anointing. From there, the Word and power of our perfect God flow from the heart of His anointed, though imperfect man or woman. It is also from this hallowed place that His plans are birthed. When we approach the altar and especially the pulpit, we should do so with that in mind. I want to be close to the front because from that perspective, if we are watching closely, God can be seen in action with human eyes.

"How God anointed Jesus of Nazareth with the Holy Ghost and with power: who went about doing good, and healing all that were oppressed of the devil; for God was with him" (Acts 10:38).

I was sitting two rows back on the close left side as Pastor Osteen spoke during one service. From that perspective, I could clearly see the conviction and love that seemed to beam from his eyes. Say what one will, but those things cannot be learned or produced by human effort. Following closely behind that conviction and love, we find God's miracle-working power. It is God who is the source of such things. On that morning so long ago, under the anointing, the pastor took his Bible in his hand, opened it to the front page, and lifted it in the air. With tears in his eyes and with the voice of authority I recall him saying, *"Open your Bible to the front page where it says, 'Holy Bible', and right under that write, 'This is for helping people,' lest you should ever forget. May everything that you do or say be done with that in mind."* The anointing of God's Holy Spirit in those words burn forever in my heart.

[3]James Taylor (vocalist), "The Water is Wide," Old Scottish Folk Song, arranged by James Taylor and Don Grolnick, track 12 on *New Moonshine,* Columbia, 1991.

5

THE BLACK HOLE

The hustle and bustle of a city the size of Houston made me long for what I knew in my childhood. I enjoyed dirt roads and country life, so when I was given the opportunity, I permanently moved to my grandfather's cabin and spent much of my young adult years living in the forest. The cabin was on heavy black gumbo bottomland surrounded by trees and dense underbrush, with the closest neighbor a quarter-mile away. A year or so after I moved there, my grandparents left their home in Houston and moved out to the woods where I lived, literally around the bend and up the hill from me. The solitude was still wonderful even with my family—a crowd of Sicilian-Jewish-Indians—that came with them.

I tried to be a good neighbor to the country folk I met. Meetings at the community center six miles away were frequented by older men in cowboy hats and boots who spent their days on horseback or on tractors and ladies in big dresses who smelled like flour and apple pie. The get-togethers were usually spent talking about politics, listening to country colloquialisms, and the dry humor of the folks living in the glens and backroads of that country since the days of the Republic of Texas. I deeply enjoyed the rich history represented among those wonderful people, and I could sit for hours and listen to their stories of cowboys, covered wagons, and Indians along the old Tyler Road. However, one evening while I was listening, an old rancher came up and sat down and said, *"How do you like livin' down in the black hole?"* I said, *"The black hole? What's that?"* He said, *"That's where you live! Everybody around here knows that place is haunted."* I shrugged my shoulders and told him that I was not worried about it, and he just patted me on the back and chuckled.

As time went by, the more I prayed in tongues, the hungrier I got for the Word of God, so I would voraciously read the Bible. The more I sought God, the more I noticed "manifestations" in the house. At first, there were sounds, like someone outside on the porch or bumps and crashes in other rooms. I would go and check and not find anything. Then, the unexplainable happenings seemed to escalate, and I would find an object that had fallen over for no reason or papers on the floor. Things like this can make a person nervous; we have all seen monster movies, which did not help my problem with fear at all! It was no fun, and it seemed like the more fear I felt, the more the manifestations would increase.

I thought I had a demon problem in the house. I never considered it was ghosts because I reasoned that if I were a dead person who wanted to cause problems, why would I hang around in the woods? Ghosts would be over in Houston or someplace where there were more people to annoy. The Bible says in 2 Corinthians 11:14, "Satan himself is transformed into an angel of light." It was only common sense that if he could transform himself into other persons or things, it was possible that he was pretending to be a ghost. So, I figured there must be a way to get rid of it.

In the Bible studies I attended from time to time, some folks told an old Pentecostal saint about what was going on at my cabin. Not knowing what to call it, I asked him if I had a "poltergeist" in the house. The person smiled and said, *"No, you just have a demon in there! Just get a can of devil spray and run that bug off. You'll recognize the can when you see it because it will say on the label: J-E-S-U-S."* I asked the person if he could come over and help me get rid of it, and he said:

> *"Well, yes, I could, but there is one problem with that. If I come over and cast it out, it will wait until I'm gone and come back angry. Besides, it is your house, so you must seek God and do it yourself. Then it will be gone for good. Don't worry; you can do it."*

The more I thought about it, somehow, the thought of a ghost seemed easier to deal with than a demon. Most people have never considered the idea of a living person, visible or not, who is actively at work, trying to find a way to murder them. This experience was my first glimpse into the reality of that situation. A demon is the epitome of evil trying to kill people, and I had one on my property and in my house! Ghosts in the classical sense do not exist, but the thought of some disembodied someone seemed more impersonal and less threatening than an evil spirit who wanted me dead. Nevertheless, it was there; it was real, and I had to get rid of it.

I started praying and specifically asking God what to do. Then, one day as I was praying, a voice whispered in my ear, *"Mark, go out in the woods and pray!"* I looked out the window and said, *"Out there? In the black hole? Not me! No!"* Ever since I had heard about the Black Hole, the deep woods seemed dark and spooky, and I needed clear land around my feet and the lights on to pray!

As time went by, the manifestations continued to increase. I realized I needed more power, so I asked God to teach me to pray as Jesus did. After that, I began to snap awake at 4 AM sharp, and I would get up and pray in tongues for two hours. God did all kinds of things to wake me up. I had no alarm clock, but I heard one ring. There was also a loud physical banging on the front door that awakened me from a sound sleep! When I got up and went to the door, no one was there. I looked all around the outside of the house, and there was not a soul to be found, but I noticed that it was 4 o'clock, so I prayed.

It was my custom to sleep on the floor on a thick carpet in front of the huge fireplace. There was no heat in the house at first, so the only way to keep warm was to be close to the fireplace in the winter. I was always concerned about the fireplace flue and tried to keep it closed when not in use because it was not unheard of for some forest creature to come down the chimney. One night, I was sound asleep, and I woke up in total darkness and clearly heard with my ears a deep, guttural growl right next to my left ear. I snapped wide awake, and I thought, *"Uh-oh! A granddaddy coon has gotten into this house!"* That may seem amusing to the reader, but a raccoon is in the bear family, and a big one can weigh 25 pounds and be as mean as a bear! I asked the Lord, *"What do I do, Father?"* When I prayed, the thing that was growling grabbed me by the throat and began to strangle me. I distinctly felt two hands around my throat. In my terror, I could not breathe and felt a paralysis come over me, and God said, *"It's a demon, just say 'Jesus.'"* I could not say anything because I could not breathe, but deep inside, I mustered my strength and forced out the word, *"Jesus!"* When I uttered the Name, the thing was immediately gone, and all that was left was silence. Just in case, I jumped up, turned on the lights, got down the .410 shotgun, and searched the house, but nothing was there.

I had been raised in almost constant fear, and I learned that it accomplishes nothing, so this bizarre encounter made me angry. I finally admitted to myself that this was the work of a demon. What nerve! Who does he think he is coming into my house? He didn't pay the bills! I never did anything to him! Maybe that place was "the black hole," but I was not putting up with that. I once heard a lady testify that when she felt fear, she would say, "*Oh!*

Mr. Devil, I don't want you here, but since you have come, let's read the Bible together!" The Bible says in the Gospel of Mark, chapter 16, that believers would cast out demons in the Name of Jesus. So, she would open her Bible to Revelation and read to the demon about his future—his final destination in the Lake of Fire. Since the devil is a coward, he always leaves in terror.

Unless he is somehow trying to involve himself in our private matters, I do not suggest that anyone go after the devil. To call out an evil spirit without the help of God can be suicidal. It is true that the devil is defeated, but if a situation does not involve my ministry, family, or business, I will not get involved with him. Without Jesus, the devil will win the fight, and the person who confronts him on their own is ill-advised and usually comes out in bad shape. However, it's different if he bothers me at home! Nothing will change if you sit there and do nothing, so I decided to put the fear away and root him out. I got on my knees, and I said:

> *"Father, in Jesus' Name, You know that I have no power over anything without You, but You said for me to cast out demons, and I have to deal with the devil and this fear, and this thing may have been in these woods for generations, so please help me get rid of him!"*

I did a thorough house cleaning and made sure there was nothing in the house to which the devil might be attached and threw away some figurines, a couple of music albums, and some odds and ends that I did not feel right about having. Finally, after asking God's help, I said out loud: *"Devil, I'm not praying to you; I am talking to you! I rebuke you in Jesus' Name! You get out of my house!"* I knew I had to face my fears, so that very night, I waited for the stroke of midnight, lit a candle, turned off all the lights, sat on the floor, and opened the Bible. I said, *"I have victory over you in Jesus' Name! You're not tough enough because I am here with the Holy Ghost. Go away and don't come back."* I read from the book of Revelation out loud. Nothing happened, and my growling adversary did not show up. After a short time, an anointing of victory came on me, and I had a mini-Holy Ghost party there in the dark. After that, I said, *"Yeah, I thought so, you coward!"*

From that night forward, there were no more manifestations in my house, and I told the ranchers and farmers at the community center that there was no more black hole because I got rid of it in Jesus' Name!

6

GOD'S FIRST AUTOMOBILE

Since I was overcoming my fears, I thought that I should obey God and go out into the woods and do some of my praying. There was a concealed thicket about 100 yards away from the house, and there were no distractions out there. I strapped on my .38 just in case I saw a snake, and I got out my chain saw, rake, and small lawnmower and cut a path through the brush and a circle of about 10 feet across. I mowed it, burned the brush, and put a lawn chair in the middle of the hollow. Unless someone knew the place or could hear me in there praying, I was invisible because the brush was thick, and it was covered from the air by a dense canopy of oaks and pecans. The forest is a wild place, so each time I went out there, I made sure that there were no copperheads around, and I regularly began to pray in my thicket.

Six months later, my pickup broke down, and I didn't know what to do. I decided that I should go out in the woods to ask God to help. I went out to the thicket, and I prayed:

> *"Father, You said in Philippians 4:19 that You would supply all of my needs according to Your riches in glory by Christ Jesus. I need a pickup because mine is broken down. I am working and doing everything I know to do, and I need Your help. So, I ask for You to pick it out. I don't care what kind as long as it runs and doesn't always break down. I would like air-conditioning, an AM/FM cassette player so I can listen to Christian music and teachings, and that it be paid for, in Jesus' Name, Amen."*

A couple of minutes after my prayer, God said, *"Go to the house."* As I was walking back to the house, I noticed someone I knew coming down the road toward the house in a blue Chevrolet El Camino. It was a 1982 model with 5,000 miles on it. The man got out, came over to me, and threw me the keys. I asked what he was doing, and he said, *"I want to give you my pickup. I feel that God wants you to have it."* I told him that I felt bad about taking his truck and asked him what he would drive. He said he was going away and couldn't take it; he wanted me to use it for Jesus. So, I took it and drove it until it had almost 100,000 miles; it served me well.

7

ANSWERING THE CALL

It is hard to support a family! Trying to make ends meet and paying attention to the family's emotional needs can be difficult. Things can get out of control if you don't watch out, and they did with me. I was self-employed and worked with trees, but I was having trouble staying busy. I couldn't pay the bills, and it seemed like everyone was angry at me. Finally, the pressure was too much, so I went up on a nearby hilltop one Sunday evening. I called out on the Lord, saying, *"God, I don't know what to do!"* He answered me immediately and said, *"Yes, you know what to do. Repent! You know enough of the gospel to save China, but you have not been putting Me first. You have put your business and your family before Me. I want all of you."* I could recognize a certain urgency in His voice, so I repented. I told Him that I would go to work for Him if He wanted, and I asked Him to lead me. I count that day, September 20, 1981, as the day that Mark Scrivener Ministries was established.

A short time later, I was driving down Interstate 45, about five minutes south of Huntsville, Texas, looking for work for my tree company. I turned on the radio, and just like he had been waiting for me, a man with a heavy Texas accent shouted on the radio, *"Need a job?!"* There was a pause like he was giving me a minute to think about it. I said to myself, *"Hey, that guy is talking to me!"* He continued, *"Go to work for God! He's hiring, and He'll pay you well! Turn that truck around, go into town. Look for a Christian Center, Christian Tabernacle, or Christian Fellowship, and go in and tell the pastor that I said God was hiring!"* As a result, I turned around and found a church matching that description! I walked in and asked to speak with the pastor. I told him *"A man on the radio said to come in here and tell you that God was hiring."* The pastor said, *"He was correct! God is indeed hiring, but He will pay you because we don't have much money!"* I said, *"Please put me to work!"*

The pastor gave me a job in the church. For orientation, he said, *"Do you see that lady over there? She is your boss. She cleans the restrooms, but she is embarrassed to clean the men's room. So go work for her."* I said to myself, *"God said to do this, so I know that He knows what He is doing, so I will do it, and I will treat these people as if they were Jesus Himself!"* This job was my introduction to ministry, and I've been serving God, doing various things with all that is in me since then.

In 2018, God told me to slow the traveling and preaching down and take a job (again) with the State of Texas working with juvenile offenders traveling to their homes and institutions statewide. I felt as if I had done something wrong. Why should I stop a coast-to-coast ministry that goes into Latin American nations to work at a secular job? I was hurt. Then in 2020, the virus and election problems happened, and many people who lived as full-time ministers were struggling. But, God had provided that job, and because of its nature, they insisted that I continue to travel. Many of the places I went to had churches that wanted me to preach. I still went to Mexico, and my boss helped finance it! So, it was all part of the plan, and we were also able to minister to some troubled youths.

Every Christian is called to service or ministry, some full-time and some part-time. If we are born-again, we are ministers of Father God, and He sees to it that everything works out for us in the pursuit of serving Him. Whether we are secularly employed or full-time ministers, we are all in that service. As we serve Him, God will lead us and guide us every step of the way, even to our heavenly reward.

The ministry is not a job, as jobs go. It is never 9-5, and you rarely get paid by a paycheck. From the beginning, it seems to have always been with me. It is as close as my own skin. It began cleaning that restroom when I was in my early twenties, and it has since become my closest relative. The ministry requires constant care. Like a child, it will call out in the night, and like a father, I must rise and care for it. As the most important thing in this life, it has cost me everything.

The ministry lives inside of my being. Without it, I have no purpose on the earth, and when my part of it is over, I will go to heaven. When I leave, the ministry will go forward through someone else's life. All ministry is bigger than anyone involved in it. This ministry and ones like it are of the utmost importance to the Lord Jesus because through them souls are saved. It has been my greatest treasure, and because of it I can do the will of God: help people.

What building has it built? What monument will be left behind to mark my short journey on this planet? There have been no buildings or monuments, but the influence that remains in every place it goes, and I trust after my passing, will be the monolith of changed lives.

8

VISITATION

I am from Texas, and everyone knows how Texans dress! A man may live in the city, but he wears a hat and boots. I lived in the country and had some land complete with a few animals, so I was confident that western wear was appropriate! First, let me say that God has nothing against western clothes; He is interested in the heart. But on one Wednesday morning, I was at my house getting ready for work. I looked at the belt buckle, and God said through the still small voice, *"Do you know why you dress the way you do? It is because you are so proud!"* That began a series of communications throughout the day in which God was dealing with me about pride. The Bible says that pride is a human problem, and it is one of the seven deadly sins, according to the Roman Catholic Church. However, like any other problem I was dealing with, I knew I had no control over it. So I took it to the Lord and prayed, *"God, I know that I am proud, but I cannot do anything about it. What do I do?"* He said, *"Go to church tonight, answer the altar call, and tell the pastor that I said you are too proud."* I had never gone to the altar at that church, but like many other things I was doing at that time, the root of my refusal to go was pride. Unbeknownst to me, it was a sign of my repentance from pride to answer the altar call.

When talking about intangible spiritual things, it is often difficult to know if something is the imagination or not. Confirmations from the Lord bring security, but only through experience can we gain basic knowledge to discern God's voice and understand how He works. We need that experience to be confident in what we are hearing so we can step out in faith. There was not always an altar call on Wednesday nights at the church I attended, so a good confirmation for this word would be if there were an altar call.

That night, the pastor dismissed the service, and for a moment, I thought my word would turn out to be my imagination because people were getting up and leaving. *But he said, "Wait, wait! I need to remember to do this! There may be someone here with a need! Is there anyone who is sick or has a need?"* So, I summoned my courage, walked down the aisle, and stood in front of him. Since that was my first time at the altar, the pastor had a surprised look on his face and said, *"What can I do for you?"* I said, *"Nothing! God told me to come up here and tell you that I am too proud."* He looked puzzled, told me to raise my hands in the air as a symbol of my surrender, and said, *"Let's see what's going on!"*

As I mentioned in the introduction, we must constantly watch because the Son of Man often comes when we are not prepared for Him. I have learned over the years that God will tell a person to do one thing when He has something else in mind, and that was true on that night. I went forward for deliverance from pride, but something else happened.

The Bible says, "Walk circumspectly, not as fools, but as wise" (Ephesians 5:15). In ***Webster's Dictionary***, one root of the word "circumspectly" insinuates to consider everything that goes on all around at all times. Based on that, I am an observer of behavior. I do not walk blindly down the street, failing to notice the things around me. Since I was trying to learn spiritual things, I watched how the pastor ministered to me. Before that night in 1982, I had never experienced "being slain in the spirit," which occurs in many Full Gospel churches. Although it is in the Bible, I had not noticed it yet, but it is based on the verse, "As soon then as he had said unto them, I am he [Jesus], they went backward, and fell to the ground" (John 18:6).

In the past, I had observed altar calls while sitting in the congregation. In my opinion, the only people who were slain in the spirit were emotional and swooned because they were getting attention. When the pastor prayed for me, he said, *"Father, in Jesus' Name..."* and without any force whatsoever, he lightly touched me on the forehead with the very tips of his fingers. Although I had never been slain in the spirit, I had experienced a few fistfights before I sold out to Jesus, and I knew what being knocked out felt like. When the pastor touched me, I like to say that God slapped some of the pride out of me. I saw stars, and my ears started ringing just like someone hit me, and with no choice in the matter, I fell back on the floor. At first, what happened to me did not feel spiritual; it felt physical! However, when I went down, I landed in what appeared to be a cloud. It was completely silent, and I could only see a white mist in front of my eyes with what seemed like a reflection of myself from above in a mirror. I remember how young and filthy I seemed standing in that place, but even then, there was an exhilarating feeling of completeness that utterly filled me. I have attempted to explain this feeling, and the only way to describe it would be to say that I had no questions, no desires, and no lack. I felt totally loved and as if my eyes were open for the first time in my life.

Looking at my life with those open eyes, it all seemed so simple! I said to myself, "*Of course! Anyone could do that!*" While I was rejoicing in that world of wonder, out of the silence from someplace in the mist, a booming male voice said, "*I have called you from your mother's womb. You will go and do...*" For what seemed like 30 minutes, God laid out the entire plan for my life! I remember seeing where I would go and what I would do throughout my ministry. But after He had spoken to me, I am ashamed to say that instead of being quiet and finding out what else was going on, still in the vision, I began to shout, "*That's wonderful! I'm going to tell everybody!*" In 2 Corinthians 12:4, Paul the apostle said he heard things in heaven that were unlawful for a man to utter. I suppose something similar happened to me because when I began to say I was going to tell everyone, I immediately felt the vision ending and the revelation slipping away.

I woke up lying on the floor, and some ushers helped me to my feet because I couldn't walk! I had to be carried to my seat, and I kept saying, *"I can't forget, I can't forget, I can't forget!"* But alas, after my head cleared the next day, the only things I could remember were that God called me, how I felt at the altar, and that I will go and do. I had to be driven home that night and was still enjoying the touch from Jesus the next morning. After a few days, I asked one of the ushers how long I was lying on the floor, and he said, *"You went down and got right back up again!"* It seemed like the entire thing lasted a half hour or so, but it all happened in a split second!

A short time after that, a Missionary Baptist Church in a rough part of Houston invited me to preach. I knew the associate pastor because his wife, "Auntie" Mae, took care of my parents' house and helped raise me during my first six years of life. They loved me as their own child and were delighted that I had answered the call to preach. When I arrived on that Sunday morning, an elderly man, bowed over from great age, came up to me and called me "The Traveler!" I had never seen the man before and never saw him again. I said, *"Yes, sir! I came down here about 80 miles from the woods!"* He said, *"Well, the Lord says that you will go much further than that!"* He was correct. I have never measured, but I am sure that I have traveled more than a million miles for the Lord Jesus, and there is still much more to come!

9

THE TITHE & THE CHICKENS

I am a sensitive person, and it is my custom to be concerned about others in traffic and crowds. I try to remember that I am not the only person on the earth; I think about how I affect others.

As a young person, I never thought much about how I dressed because no one seemed to care. But, I had never been exposed to the unique culture found in the Pentecostal/Charismatic circles of East Texas. People seemed to dress differently, so I was nervous about my appearance, not wanting to offend anyone. However, the sign on the front door of the church said to come as you are, so I did. I usually dressed in my best blue jeans with a belt and big buckle, shiny boots, a western shirt with a collar and long sleeves, and my denim jacket. I wore a hat, but the first time I came in the door wearing it, an usher showed me where to hang it, so I usually left that in the pickup.

With that in mind, one Sunday morning, as the pastor began to preach, he said, *"I am sorry folks, but I am going to wait until after I preach to pick up the offering because I feel that God has led me to talk about the tithe."* Due to my sensitivity about appearance and ignorance of the Bible verses that I had not yet read, I thought he said he was going to talk about (neck) ties. Ties were definitely not part of my wardrobe! I did not know what that had to do with the offering, but I felt embarrassed and buttoned the top button of my shirt. I am sure that I blushed because when the pastor saw my reaction, he said, *"I am not talking about a necktie; I am talking about 10% of our income given to God."*

When the pastor corrected me, I was relieved about my clothes, but I had never heard the word "tithe" in my life! Sure, God was good to me, but I wanted to be good to God. Besides, I wondered why I never seemed to have enough money; no matter how hard I tried, I could not get ahead! The pastor preached from a part of the Bible I had not yet studied that said:

> Will a man rob God? Yet ye have robbed me. But ye say, Wherein have we robbed thee? In tithes and offerings. Ye are cursed with a curse: for ye have robbed me, even this whole nation. Bring ye all the tithes into the storehouse, that there may be meat in mine house, and prove me now herewith, saith the LORD of hosts, if I will not open you the windows of heaven, and pour you out a blessing, that there shall not be room enough to receive it. And I will rebuke the devourer for your sakes, and he shall not

> destroy the fruits of your ground; neither shall your vine cast her fruit before the time in the field, saith the LORD of hosts (Malachi 3: 8-11).

I was amazed that was in the Bible! When Malachi got to the part that said, *"You are cursed with a curse,"* I thought to myself, *"No wonder I can't get ahead! I'm living in disobedience!"* Based on that Scripture, the pastor took up the offering. My earnings during the previous week were $200, and I had my last $22 in my pocket. I hurriedly got $20 and put it in the offering.

It was not until the offering bucket was gone that I thought, *"Wait a minute! How am I going to live all week on $2?"* That week turned out to be the most blessed week I have ever spent serving God, and I never lacked anything. Somehow or another, everything I needed that week seemed to appear from every direction, and the following Sunday, I still had that remaining $2 in my wallet! I could not figure it out, but it worked, and after almost 40 years, I still cannot figure it out. I discovered something that has been a source of blessing to me all my life—something I cannot live without. Tithing works because God said it would, and a tither lives in a blessing that can never be explained but is indispensable in life!

I learned about the blessings of the tither during my years in the forest. With a pond covering about one-fifth of an acre, I had water and enough land to have a few animals. There were, of course, dogs and cats, but I also had a couple of cattle, a horse or two, a Sicilian donkey named Jezebel, a milk goat named Hannah, two geese with an attitude, several ducks, and at my best, I had about 30 chickens, not counting the three roosters. My grandfather and I had put together a hen house with boxes where the hens could lay their eggs. At first, to start my little chicken business, I bought about 40 pullets (baby chickens) and raised them in a wire cage in the hen house. The idea was to keep them in the cage so that snakes and birds did not get them until they were large enough to fend for themselves. One afternoon I looked at my pullets, and they looked sick. They were not very big, but they seemed cramped inside the cage, and I was afraid that they would die, so I decided it was time to let them out. The minute I let them out, a thought occurred to me that was a bit foreign. It said, *"What if a wolf gets them?"* I immediately remembered the Scripture in Malachi 3 that said, *"I will rebuke the devourer for your sakes, and he shall not consume the fruits of your ground."* I said aloud:

> *"Satan, even though this applies to anyone who receives any good thing in life, this Scripture in Malachi was talking to farmers. If there ever was an area where that would work, this is one of them! So, satan, you be gone in Jesus' Name because I am a tither, and God said He would rebuke you, so you leave my chickens alone."*

My house was in a clearing in the forest. I had witnessed to most of my neighbors, so they knew that I was a Holy Ghost Christian. In general, they thought that I was strange. There were a couple of neighbors who lived a quarter-mile away. From one person's breakfast table, if you squinted, my clearing was visible through the thicket, even though the house could not be seen.

One morning about a week after letting the chickens out of their cage, I went to town to take care of some business. After I came home later that afternoon, a neighbor called me on the party line in a concerned way and said,

> *"I saw something strange today through the trees in the clearing by your house. I didn't go down there, but it looked as big as a moving van. It was a white color so bright that you would think it would be in a science fiction movie, and I could make it out moving slowly in the clearing. I wanted to know if you saw any tracks on the ground because I don't know what that was. Were you expecting anyone today? I thought it looked like a UFO!"*

Later, I looked outside and saw no tracks or disturbances on the ground. After listening to my neighbor, I could not imagine what it may have been. I was sure that it was not a flying saucer, but I remembered I had read where angels sometimes traveled in chariots—one even picked up Elijah in the Old Testament. So, I called her back and said, *"I don't see any tracks on the ground, and I don't know what it was, but maybe it was a chariot of angels doing something."* The person scoffed and abruptly hung up. I have always been curious about the worldly mind! They are quick to believe in UFOs, ghosts, and incredible phenomena like that, but if someone says something about God or angels, they scoff and write them off as insane!

When I pondered about what that vehicle might have been, I sat down and prayed and said, *"God, if that was an angelic operation of some kind, what were they doing?"* He said one word: *"Chickens!"* I jumped back in shock! I thought that if He would do that for a bunch of chickens, what would He do if it were something really important to me? During my time in the chicken business, even though I lived deep in the forest full of animals of all kinds, I usually gathered 25-30 eggs per day and never lost a hen until it was time for me to leave home and go to the world with the gospel.

10

THE UNDISCOVERED COUNTRY[4]

In the days before people brought lights and noise to my forest, I enjoyed climbing on the roof of the house to lay on my back and watch the stars when there was no moon. The pitch darkness made the Milky Way shine in a brilliant splendor that caused the eternity in my heart to seem like a realm that I could readily touch. I found myself moved to emotion as I dreamt of worlds in between the vast distances along those unknown astral highways.

Since I began to pray in tongues, I noticed a curious drawing-away on the inside. There is a destination to which we are all bound. It seems as if very few really want to go, but it is unavoidable. Even though it is not that far from where we are now, we never seem to arrive no matter how long we travel. That place exists only in the ethereal world of our imagination, and we call it "the future." Tomorrow is a realm where we will see wonders beyond description and meet new people, but we can only get there if we go away from where we are now.

I cannot understand how anyone could be satisfied with life on this planet in the 21st Century! More than anything, I wanted to explore new worlds! I usually say, *"I was born 100 years too late or 100 years too early."* Had I been born earlier in history, I could have taken part in the exploration of the West, and if I had been born later, I could have gone to explore Mars or warped away on something like the Starship Enterprise. I even had a bumper sticker on my car that said, "Beam me up, Scotty! There's no intelligent life down here!" People thought that my bumper sticker was funny, but deep in my heart, I was serious. I was so bored with life! I felt like a young Alexander the Great lamenting because he thought that his father, Phillip, had seized so much territory that there would be no new worlds to conquer! Everyplace on Earth had been seen, and there was nothing new, and that curious drawing-away seemed to grow stronger with each passing day.

I prayed about everything. So one day, I said to the Lord:

> *"God, I'm sad! I have a longing on the inside, and I always thought that in the future, somehow I would be given a chance to get off this planet and explore Mars or the stars, but that doesn't seem like something I will ever be able to do!"*

God's response to my statement shook me. He said, *"Captain Kirk has got nothing on Me! Who do you think gave you that desire? And unlike the world, I will give you the desires of your heart!"* When God spoke to me that way, it caused great excitement because I knew that if ***He*** were the Source of the desire, I would be allowed to go someday. At that early date, I had no idea how it would work out, but I started small and decided to leave my ordinary behind and embrace the unknown.

One day shortly after that, I had a three-dimensional open vision while praying. In that vision, I was standing in the forest looking at a pine tree stump about 12 inches in diameter. I walked around it, pulling at the exposed roots with my hands while struggling to get that stump out of the ground. As I pondered the vision and how to remove the stump, the Holy Spirit said, *"You can't do it that way, Mark! You've got to dig it deep!"* I immediately snapped out of it and was back in the house.

I thought about the vision, and being someone accustomed to working with trees, I knew that a pine tree a foot in diameter would have a height of about 20 feet. Pine trees have what is known as a tap root, and that root goes down into the ground to a depth of about one-third its height. To remove the tree completely, you would have to dig down six feet!

I asked God what He meant by that vision, and He said, *"The Bible is like the pine tree stump, you can see a small part on the surface, and there is more beneath the surface than is visible. If you are going to get to most of it, you just can't scratch the surface. You have to dig deep."*

I did not know how to study the Bible in a deeper way than I had been doing already, so I went to a Bible store and asked. They suggested a ***Strong's Concordance***, a

Greek-English interlinear Bible, and a Greek lexicon. I bought those books and soon discovered that I could not make hide nor hair out of the Greek language to use the lexicon. Since the New Testament is written in Greek, I knew God spoke Greek. So, I got up early one morning and asked Him to help me with the Greek language enough to use the lexicon. By faith, I sat down at the kitchen table with a pencil and paper, got out the lexicon, wrote down the Greek alphabet, and in two hours, I had enough knowledge of Greek to use the lexicon and pronounce what I was reading! I am not saying that I can read Greek, but I can pronounce the words and look them up in a dictionary.

I continued to study very hard, and even with all my effort, I still felt the pulling-away on the inside. The more I learned, the more I desired to be out doing the works of Christ, especially because Mark 16 says to go into all the world and preach the gospel to every creature. So, I thought long and hard about it, and in so doing, I found my new worlds to conquer, but I did not know how to leave.

I had a friend in West Texas who was a farmer, and he was gifted in the prophetic. Since God talked to him, I called and asked him for advice. He said, *"Why don't you start by going to Bible school? That way, you could leave and study at the same time!"* I said, *"That is a great idea, but where would I go?"* He suggested Rhema Bible Training Center in Tulsa, Oklahoma, but I told him that I did not want to start by going that far away. He then said, *"Why don't you go talk to Pastor Osteen in Houston? I heard that*

Lakewood Church is starting a Bible School." I told him that maybe I should do that, and he said, *"I am going to pray for you to have favor so you can do it."* He prayed and hung up.

Pastor Osteen was a friend of my grandparents, so it's possible that he might have had my address. Still, on the **very next day**, I received a personal letter in the mailbox on Lakewood stationery, signed by Pastor Osteen, asking me to come to his office and included a number to call. I placed the call and set up an appointment for the next day. I was very curious about the letter because I had not had time to say anything to anyone about the conversation with my farmer friend; it had been less than 24 hours since he and I had talked.

I could not imagine what a man as famous as Pastor Osteen would want with me. Since my grandparents knew him, I asked them to go with me. We arrived at Lakewood, spoke to the receptionist, and were called to the pastor's office. He had us sit on his sofa, and after the pleasantries, he asked me what he could do for me. I said, *"Pastor, you wrote me a letter and asked me to come in."* He said, *"I did? Do you have it?"* I gave him the letter; he read it and said, *"That's my letter! Do you know what I wanted?"* I said, *"No, Pastor! I have no idea!"* He said, *"Well, then what can I do for you?"* I told him that my farmer friend in West Texas told me they were opening a Bible School, and I would like to go to it. He said, *"Why yes! We are opening a Bible school in the Fall of 1983, but I don't think we have formally announced it yet."* I asked if he would approve of my attending, and he said he would. He told me to ask his secretary to send me an application once they were printed.

Did God want *me* to go to Bible School? I have always had a problem with my self-image. I know me! I am the guy in the mirror, and he is that person who was always getting into trouble, with little or no knowledge of how he got there. In the Christian circles I frequented, I never felt I could measure up most of the time. My problem with self-worth was caused by being trapped in a religious circle of deception often found among pew-warmers of the western world. Our concept of what is good and bad comes from our point of view, and when we do not venture more than 20 miles from home, our point of view can be very limited. To break free from that circle, we must begin to look at things through the eyes of the Holy Spirit and be able to get away from what is comfortable to our flesh.

The thought of going back to the big city without knowing anything about how I was to live and support myself was difficult. I had grown accustomed to the quiet isolation of life in the forest; it seemed strange to be suddenly thrust into a crowd.

I left my home in the late summer of 1983 and never went back, except to visit. It was sad to pull out on that dirt road and see my grandparents standing in the driveway with tears in their eyes, waving goodbye. But with the stars as my eventual destination, my traveling ministry began on that day as I drove away from the forest. My pursuit of a deeper walk in the supernatural began with my study at Lakewood Bible Institute on

August 29, 1983. As time went by, I learned that Christians who follow the Holy Ghost many times must leave home to follow the path God has prepared for us in the keeping of the faith and eventually go beyond the clouds!

Leaving is part of this life, so instead of avoiding the inevitable, I learned to run toward it. In so doing, my tomorrows have become my Promised Land. In that world, I am always satisfied with my Lord and Savior, Jesus Christ, but never satisfied with the status quo. I am always at home in and with the Holy Ghost, but never at home in the flesh to the extent that I allow roots to go down too far. I always long to be at home, but to arrive I must go!

[4]William Shakespeare, "Hamlet," Act 3, Scene 1 (1603), In the Public Domain.

11

CHRIST IN ME

> To whom God would make known what is the riches of the glory of this mystery among the Gentiles; which is Christ in you, the hope of glory (Colossians 1: 27).

When I drove away from home and left my grandparents, I felt a sadness in my heart, like I had lost a friend. Therefore, when I arrived at Lakewood Church, I went directly into the prayer room to seek God. When I sat down and prayed in the Holy Ghost, an overpowering, supernatural peace flooded me almost immediately. It made me understand that even though I had never before stepped into this future and did not know what it held, I made the right choice.

I went to school early every day to spend time in that prayer room. After a while in Bible school, I noticed I started having a burden or a heavy feeling, and I did not know why. When trying to be sensitive to the Holy Spirit, there is no way to be sure about what is going on without taking an active role. Unless God tells you to sit around, sitting around never accomplishes anything, so I applied myself to prayer in the Holy Ghost over my burden.

One day, I was walking and praying in tongues about my burden, and I said, *"Jesus, please tell me once and for all, what is this about?"* I would like to say that I heard a still small voice, but that would be an understatement because I "felt" the words as Jesus answered me. Everyone has felt the vibration in their throats and heads produced by the movement of their vocal cords when they are speaking. After I asked what the burden was about, I "felt" in the area of my solar plexus, just below my diaphragm, the words, *"I want homosexuals."*

Sometimes when we speak about having Jesus in our hearts, we think nice religious thoughts about stained glass windows, church pews, sweet hymns, and people in backward collars. When confronted with reality, it sometimes is hard to shake people from their religious mindsets! When I heard the voice, I got very excited, not so much about what He said, but that He had said it from inside me! I was elated.

People with me saw my excitement and were curious about what had happened, and I said, *"Jesus lives in me! He's inside of me!"* And sure enough, they were pulled away into the religious mindsets and said, *"Oh, how sweet! The boy just realized that he is saved!"* I said, *"No! You don't understand! Of course, I'm saved, but I am not talking about being saved! Jesus talked to me, and His voice came from inside me! I felt it!"*

It is true that someday when we die, we will go to heaven, but I am talking about the present-day reality of the Son of God living inside us! That is the mystery of Colossians! The Lord Jesus will live inside normal human beings and use our bodies as His vehicle to finish the job, as the Messiah within! The voice came out of me because that is where He lives, and I am His Temple!

The reality of Christ in us is what Christians often have a hard time understanding. Let's imagine for a moment: What would it be like to have the Lord Jesus with us in the flesh at home in our guest bedroom? If He were staying at our house with us, and we woke up sick, would we go to the doctor? Would we dig around in the medicine cabinet for the right pill, or would we knock on the bedroom door and tell Him about it? That's right; one touch from His hand and all sickness is banished from our bodies.

If we received a huge electric bill, what would we do if Jesus were in the back bedroom? Would we call the boss and ask for overtime to pay the bill, or would we knock on the door and tell Him about it? Remember the Scripture when Jesus needed money to pay the bill for the Temple tax? His response was to send Peter fishing! What a great boss! I would not like doing a lot of overtime to pay a light bill, but I would go fishing anytime! The first fish that came up would have the money in its mouth, and then we keep on fishing!

If satan knocked on the front door and wanted to cause problems and Jesus was in the back bedroom, what would we do? Would we call the pastor to come over and cast out the devil? Would we ask for counseling? Once again, we would tell the devil that someone in the back bedroom would like to talk to him. We would call out, *"Oh, Lord Jesus! Someone at the front door wants to talk to You!"* And then we would forget about it and leave it up to our guest.

How would our church service be on Sunday if Jesus were our visitor at home? On Sunday morning, we would get up to the smell of breakfast cooking, and the Lord Jesus would be our chef. Afterward, He would say, *"Let's get ready for church!"* He would go with us to the service, and when people found out that Jesus of Nazareth was there in person at our church, life as we know it would cease to exist! The hospitals for miles around would empty with people bringing the sick. No matter which religion people belonged to, they would come because of the power pouring out of His nail-scarred hands. The army would block the nearest freeway as Air Force One landed, and the President and his cabinet would disembark and go by motorcade to our little church to see Jesus. Before coming in, they would go to the flagpole and politely lower the flag of the United States and fold it and come down the aisle on their knees and lay it at His feet because the King has come! Her Royal Highness, the Queen of Great Britain, would arrive with her consort, and she would kneel and lay her crown at His feet. The world would change! Suddenly the world's attention would be off of life-in-general and be on Him! Jesus is here!

Those are wonderful things to imagine, but what Jesus said is more incredible than that!

> Nevertheless I tell you the truth; It is expedient for you that I go away: for if I go not away, the Comforter will not come unto you; but if I depart, I will send him unto you (John 16:7).

Jesus said that it was good for us if He went away! Even though it would be so wonderful for Jesus to be with us in His flesh, that is not what God is trying to achieve. God wants to work through the church! It stands to reason that if the world would drastically change by Jesus being here with us in the flesh, we should expect similar results with the body of Christ through the power of the Holy Ghost on the inside.

When the Holy Spirit told me that He wanted homosexuals, it was during the time of a well-known festival in Houston that gay people from all over the country attended. I told God that I would attempt to obey Him. I sought permission from the Bible School, and the Dean of Students allowed a group of about 15 students to go preach the gospel in the streets.

As we were leaving, a fellow Bible student walked up to me and said, "*God said to learn Proverbs 3:25-26 because you will need it out there.*" It reads, "Be not afraid of sudden fear, neither of the desolation of the wicked, when it cometh. For the Lord shall be thy confidence, and shall keep thy foot from being taken." By that time in my life, fear was no longer a major issue for me. Fear does not seem to bother me when my life is in danger for Jesus. The fear that bothered me is usually rooted in my issues, not His assignments, so I did not understand how that Scripture applied to our little missionary endeavor.

We preached the gospel up and down the street that night, and other than being spit on and a little name-calling, we had few results. However, at 2 AM, the bars closed, and people began to gather. Our group was standing on a street corner with a block wall on our left; to our right and back, there was a large group of onlookers. In front of us, a crowd of about 50 men gathered and began to shout insults.

The situation kept escalating until the men shouting insults began to pick up rocks and started throwing them at us! The men in our group made a circle around the ladies to protect them, and I thought, *"Wow! This is not going to look good in the Houston newspaper! The headlines will say, 'Street Preachers Stoned to Death During Festival.'"* I felt the pain of a couple of rocks as they hit my arms, but with no warning, from the right, a man came pushing his way through the crowd. He was about 5'9" and wearing blue jeans and a white tee-shirt. He seemed like anyone else out there that night, but he placed himself between the angry mob and us, pointed his finger at the ones throwing rocks, and shouted, *"You stop right there! These people are here sharing the gospel of God with you! They are trying to show you the way of salvation! Listen to them!"* He then turned and smiled, looked me right in the eye, and said, *"You walk in love toward these guys because some of them like to start trouble."* As quickly as he appeared, he immediately pushed through the crowd and was gone, and I never saw him again.

The whole thing seemed like a blur. The crowd began to scatter, and some ran in terror down the street. Only 10 or 15 men remained, and they were weeping with their hands covering their faces. We went over to them and began to lead them to the Lord. There were two who stuck with us and asked us to take them to church. The following Wednesday, I drove back to that part of town to take one of the men to Lakewood Church, and he came out of his house identifying as a woman. I silently prayed, *"Jesus, you're going to have to look out for me because I'm going to take this guy to church!"* That night when Pastor Osteen issued the altar call, he ran to the altar, dedicated his life to Jesus; he returned the following Sunday dressed as a man.

I was asked to tell that testimony in church, and afterward, one man came over and said, *"You know who the man that rescued you in the street was, don't you?"* I said, *"No, I never saw him before or after, and he looked like everyone else!"* He said, *"The Bible says, 'Be not forgetful to entertain strangers: for thereby some have entertained angels unawares'" (Hebrews 13:2).* I have thought about that incident, and I am sure the man who appeared that night probably was an angel. He was not physically large, but he seemed to exert power over the crowd that was not normal, that struck terror in their hearts!

I realized that this is what Jesus meant when He said that it was expedient for us if He went away. Had He been there, we would not have experienced the results of the Messiah **inside**, nor would we have been allowed to share in His sufferings.

Since that incident, I have noticed that I have favor with homosexuals. When I am in their company, they have no fear of me, even after finding out that I am a preacher. It seems as if they want to hear what I have to say. For many years, I did not understand why homosexuals seemed to be drawn to me. However, twenty years after this incident, I was sharing the testimony at a church, and someone said, *"Don't you see? When Jesus told you that He wanted homosexuals, He wasn't talking about an anointing that would be there for that festival and then be gone; it was to be with you for life!"* I believe that to be true, and it is a pleasure to minister to whomever, wherever God sends me. It is true that Jesus loves people, no matter who they are or what they do.

12

LEARNING SPANISH

It is customary for Bible Colleges to ask students to work in a church or other ministry, doing something for Jesus as part of their Christian service. While at Lakewood Bible Institute, I helped in the usher ministry during church services.

When I left the forest and went to Lakewood, I did not exactly know what God wanted me to do in the ministry. I went away in obedience and expected Him to let me know while I was there. To help myself hear when God spoke to me, I fasted three days one week, two days the next week, and one day the third week.

Houston, like all of Texas, has a sizeable Hispanic population. Due to my upbringing on our southern border, it was a great revelation when I found out that everyone who speaks Spanish is not necessarily from Mexico. Many different countries on Earth speak

Spanish. Although the language sounds the same to the non-Spanish speaker, the various dialects of Spanish and the customs of each country can be *very* different.

One evening while ushering at Lakewood, I was standing between two men who were both speaking Spanish. Because I did not speak Spanish at the time, it sounded like gibberish to me. When they finished, one of the men pointed to the other and said, *"He doesn't speak Spanish!"* I responded by saying, *"Whatever he was saying sounded good to me!"* He said, *"He's from Houston, and for you to understand his Spanish, you have to speak both English and Spanish because sometimes what he says is closer to English than Spanish. In my country, we speak 'Castellano,' which is pure Spanish, and English won't help you!"* The man speaking was from South America.

While listening to their conversation, not understanding anything, I noticed a very "quiet" feeling deep inside of my midsection that seemed somehow like a tender love, like weeping on the inside. It was very subtle. Had I not been fasting, I do not know if I would have noticed it. The feeling continued over a long period of time. Since I was seeking God to tell me what to do in the ministry, I thought that maybe I should talk to someone who could help me decipher my feelings.

Lakewood would not tell anyone what to do with their ministries and expected each person to go to God and decide on their own, but they would help. The Dean of Students suggested that I speak with the Missions Director, so I met with him one afternoon. I explained to him that I was listening to someone speaking Spanish and had a feeling of love and weeping on the inside, and while I was talking to him, I began to cry. He said, *"Brother Mark, we at Lakewood do not like to tell anyone what to do, but I have seen this before. I believe that God is calling you to Latin America and that He wants you to learn Spanish."* I asked him if he knew of a Spanish language school, and he said that there was one in McAllen, Texas, known as *Kingsway Missionary Institute.*

I prayed and asked God, and He told me to go to Kingsway, so the following year, I attended that school and began to learn the Spanish language, Latin American psychology, and customs.

McAllen was in a part of Texas known as the Rio Grande Valley. It was a beautiful place with citrus groves, tall palm trees, tropical flowers and sombreros. While at Kingsway, part of the curriculum was attending a Spanish language church to accustom our ears to the language and expose us to the culture. They presented us with a list of churches in the area, and I looked it over. However, I understood that just as I came to Kingsway by seeking the Lord, God probably had a church already picked out for me, so I prayed, *"Father, I want to obey, so please show me where to go."*

If I pray and do not get an immediate answer, that usually means He will respond some other way, so I began to watch for Him to speak. A week or so later, I was driving down a street and felt my attention drawn to a house on the side of the road. When I looked at it, God said, *"Go there."* But, I drove past it and said, *"God! That's somebody's house! I can't just walk up to someone's private home and say, 'God told me to come here!' They'll call the police!"* After getting about half a mile down the road, I started getting a sick feeling inside that told me I was not being obedient, so I thought, *"Oh well, I had better do it. What can happen?"* I turned the car around and pulled into the driveway. From a closer perspective, I saw a small building next door that was invisible from the road; it looked like it could be a farmer's warehouse or a small church. I took a deep breath, walked up to the front door, and knocked. A young girl about twelve years of age answered, and I said, *"I am so sorry for bothering you, but is this a church?"* She said, *"Yes."*

Although I had driven down Rogers Road in that town before, I had never noticed that house! I asked the young lady, *"Is the pastor in?"* She said, *"Yes, he's around back working."* I thanked her and walked around back. I found a tall Mexican man in his yard beside the church building wearing a big sombrero. Some chickens were standing around him, and he was tossing out feed for them. I said, *"Pardon me, sir. Please forgive the intrusion, but are you the pastor?"* He responded that he was, and I walked up to him and put out my hand to shake hands. When he took my hand, I said:

> *"Sir, I don't know if you believe in speaking in tongues or not, but last year I went to Lakewood Bible Institute in Houston, and God called me to be a missionary to Latin America, and I am down here learning Spanish. The school has a rule for us to graduate that we must*

> *attend a Spanish-speaking church. I was going down the road, and I think God told me to come here!"*

I had never met the pastor and was unaware of his life and needs. But, God knows us all, and He directs our lives down the path that will help us fulfill that calling and continue to help others. When I finished talking, the man dropped his chicken feed, threw both of his hands in the air, and began to shout, *"Hallelujah! I just called Lakewood last week and asked them to send me a missionary. They said that they didn't tell people where to go, but they would pray for me, and here you are! Did Brother Osteen send you?"* I told him that he did not send me and I was just following the Holy Ghost. I let him know that I was there to give to him and not to take.

The pastor's name was Rev. Magdaleno Cruz, Jr., and his ministry was *Jesus Christ the Healer Church and Revivals.* He had been R.W. Shambach's Spanish language translator for his tent crusades in the Valley.

I worked closely with Brother Cruz and became his personal assistant and held his coat throughout the years. I grew to love that man as my own father. I served alongside him constantly for two years, and then off and on until his sad passing on December 31, 2011. I miss him greatly!

I sat at his feet and learned faith and ministry from him. I saw so many miracles in the tent crusades and at the church, and I gave and gave and gave. I never asked him for money (even though I have nothing against that) because when I gave, God gave to me! I supported my family with no visible way to do it. I learned Spanish and faith from him. I also learned the **secret of ministry**: keep going throughout the storms, crying, fears, and persecution.

13

GOD'S FAITHFUL SUPPLY

I gave up my "career" for Jesus, but in my case, I cannot say that it was giving up a lot. Before selling out to Christ, my experience in the secular world was challenging to say the least. I tell people all the time that if they do not enjoy much success working, maybe there is something beneath the surface that they do not see! Like it was with me, could it be that they are called of God? Answering God's call does not mean that a person stops working; it just means that the job stops being the focus of life and the means of support. The job stops being the career, and Jesus becomes the career.

Since selling out to Jesus and His ministry, I have performed all kinds of jobs, but they were never my source. For me, doing a job temporarily to help pay the ministry's bills stopped being a stigma or failure and became part of the plan. If a job comes along, it always turns out to be a happy time and usually serves as a wedge that gives the ministry access into a particular region for a higher purpose. Jobs have taken me into places where God wanted to start a church or similar organization, and when the ministry goal was completed, the job ended.

Pastor John Osteen used to say, *"There are three words that we can use to describe ministry. They are: work, work, work. Many times, ministry is paid for by our own secular-type labor, and with God's help, the ministry eventually begins to pay the bills."* In my case, that has been true.

Mark Scrivener Ministries, Inc. is a 501c3 evangelistic association whose corporation papers were filed in 1984 and finally incorporated in 1985. The ministry has paid the bills through the years and, often, with the help of various jobs. I operated my chicken business, cleared land, and worked on trees. I was the head wrangler at a Christian ranch and a waiter in restaurants. I worked with at-risk youth and served as a drug and alcohol counselor through a secular organization. I was interim Executive Director of a faith-based agency helping at-risk individuals become Christian, tax-paying citizens. I worked for almost three years as a juvenile parole officer. On three different occasions, I have been a professor at Bible Institutes and Colleges. I drove a tractor and worked as a farmer, hauling grain to market. The **secret to success in the ministry** is to work at whatever God gives while not neglecting the true call, which is the pulpit. I have lived exclusively from the ministry on many occasions, and I have deeply enjoyed those times. However, a job is not a setback; it is a stepping-stone on to better things.

I enjoy being comfortable, and like my daddy used to say, *"It takes money to be that way."* The question then becomes: How do I pay the bills? We work and do everything we can, but then we must count on the help that only comes from God; He is our source. Many times, seeing Him supply our needs is a hands-on way to keep sharp and see proof of God in our natural world.

I pray for many people in prayer lines, and one common thing that I hear people say is, *"I feel that God told me to do something, but it is impossible! I don't know if it's Him because I could never pay for that! I don't have the education or the finances!"* Although that seems terrifying, it is good news because the impossibility of something is usually a strong clue that it could be from God. He is the God of the impossible! Even though we are the ones with hands and feet on the earth, He will do the work through us and then pay for it. So, if I think God wants me to do a project, and I have the wherewithal to do it, I must question whether it is God because He usually asks me for things that are too much for me.

For much of my life, I have believed for finances for my family and ministry because God wants us to depend on Him as our source. It seems like every time I get comfortable, He moves me on to the next thing. His great love compels our complete obedience, where all needs will be met. Money is a necessary thing. If there is ever any doubt, a simple visit to a gasoline station without money or a credit card will be convincing enough. I think it is funny, but I have heard it said in some church meetings, *"God says that we shouldn't love money, but He doesn't say anything about liking it really well! Let's face it, we need it, and we need a lot of it to live, pay bills, and finance ministry."* I am not a materialistic person, and I believe excess materialism is wrong. Still, I want to obey God and take care of my responsibilities, and God is the source of that ambition.

I love those that God has given me. Oftentimes, I have awakened in the wee hours of the morning and observed my sleeping loved ones, and I have felt the compassion of the Holy Spirit flow toward them. I sense their helplessness and dependency upon Jesus, but I remember that I am the one that He sent to them. I am required to be a good husband and father. If they suffer, their suffering must be for Jesus; I must do everything to keep them from suffering on my account. I realize, however, that I could never supply their needs because Paul the apostle said, "But **my God shall supply** all of your needs" (Philippians 4:19). He is the only true source, but I must obey Him and utilize what He places in my hands.

I was deeply in prayer and fellowship with God one day. On the mantle in my house, there were a couple of family photos, and God suddenly spoke to me and said, *"Mark, do you know what My greatest desire is?"* I said, *"I suppose for people to be saved, Lord."* He said:

> *"Yes, but the purpose for them to be saved is so that I can participate in what you call 'family.' My greatest desire is to be a face in one of those pictures on your mantle. I want to be a member of your family. I want to go*

> *on family outings and be a guest for a family dinner. I want to be one of you!"*

The Bible says, "...the Father of our Lord Jesus Christ, Of whom the whole family in heaven and earth is named" (Ephesians 3:14-15). God is a family man, so He is the origin of parenthood and responsibility.

Responsibility is an interesting subject. We all know couples who met as children, some as young as elementary school age, and it seemed as if they knew right from the beginning that they should be together, and they decided to marry and have children. Before they even know their children, they begin to practice family planning. Love will sometimes propel a young man into a jewelry store where he will inadvisedly indebt himself to buy the perfect engagement ring. Then as they are planning their marriage, the couple decides upon a home with enough space and plans to decorate a bedroom or two in the appropriate colors with the right furnishings. They research and buy different insurance policies to protect them from any unseen calamities. They open savings accounts as they settle in their hearts that those children are their responsibility. They will do whatever is necessary, even unto death, to ensure the child will be cared for in any given situation. They hope for the best but are prepared for whatever may come.

God wanted a large family and decided to create one, but like any good parent, He practiced family planning and decided to have an insurance policy. He said in His heart, *"Even unto the killing of My Own Son, I will be responsible for My children."* The Bible refers to Jesus as "the Lamb slain from the foundation of the world" (Revelation 13:8). From the foundation of the world, before creating anything, Jesus was slain. Jesus was God's family planning and the insurance policy chosen before creating us. If we look at it that way, the whole thing becomes easier to understand!

Since God understands our need to take care of our families, businesses, ministries, and churches, it is no surprise that He says He will give seed for us to sow and then multiply our seed sown! Without His direct intervention, it would be impossible to live the supernatural life and pay the bills.

14

A SPECIAL PROVISION

One day while studying Spanish in my second year of Bible school, the Lord said, *"Mark, your family needs a day off and some time away."* I said, *"God, I don't have any money. I need You to help me if You want me to take them someplace."* He led me to decide how much a day at a zoo would cost. I sat down and calculated the cost of gasoline, food, and admission, and I made plans and told everyone that I was taking them on an outing the following Saturday at 1 PM. I prayed, *"God, you told me that my family needs time away, so I want to obey You. Based on what You told me, I need $75 above what I need to live, and I need it by next Saturday at 1 PM, in Jesus' Name."*

Seventy-five dollars, according to today's standard, does not sound like a lot of money, but it was a lot to me then, and I had no way of getting it. It was just out of my reach. I never told anyone about my need because I felt bad about involving others at that early stage in my ministry. In my opinion, it is not wrong to ask for help, but on that occasion, I felt that was not what God wanted. Every Monday, a church in the area would give me an offering based upon how much they had received in the offerings. It was a different amount every week. I needed about $60 per week to live, so I naturally thought that the pastor would give me $135 that week, but when I went into his office, I only received $20. I felt the pressure increase, but I continued to pray and thank God for the money.

I had a 1982 El Camino with a 302 V-8 engine. The gas mileage was 18 miles per gallon on a good day. On that Monday, the car was empty, so I put in eight gallons of gasoline and bought $10 worth of chicken wieners and bread from the grocery store, and then I was out of money. I said to myself, *"No problem, someone will invite me to help them do a job, or the money will come in some other way in plenty of time!"* Not including the other places I had to go, I had to drive 50 miles every day to school and back, and I had to go five times before our trip on Saturday. I went to school, the store, and two or three church services, and no one gave me anything. At the meetings, I tried to help God out by sitting close to the people I knew that were givers! I thought that God might speak to someone, but He did not.

By Wednesday afternoon, the gas gauge read "E," and on that same day, the needle on the gauge stopped moving while going around corners, meaning it was empty. That night, I was at a church service, and the owner of a large company asked me to give him a ride to his home, which was about five miles out of my way. I was sure that he would hear from God and help me out. He even invited me into his beautiful home to greet his family, but he did not give anything. I drove 50 miles on Thursday and Friday with the gas gauge sitting on "E."

On Saturday morning, I woke up with a feeling of horrible anxiety. I said, *"God, today's the day, and I don't have any gas, much less the money to go to the zoo! What do I do?"* The school held classes from Tuesday through Saturday from 8 AM to Noon, with Sunday and Monday off. God said, *"The reason you are here is to go to school, so now you do your part and go, and I will handle the rest."* I drove the speed limit all the way to school because I did not want to do anything to affect the anointing. At noon, I sat in the parking lot because I was sure that someone had not obeyed God and would come running out the door waving $75, but nothing happened, and after 15 minutes, I left. As I drove the 25 miles back to the house, I felt hopeless. By that time, I was obviously driving on a miracle because the car had been out of gas since the previous Wednesday! There was no one I could ask... but God.

On the highway back, I felt sick to my stomach. The financial pressure was terrible. What if I run out of gas? Because it was the days before cell phones, I wondered how I would get to a pay phone? Where would I get a quarter for the phone? Who would I call to tell that God had failed me? Was I crazy? What do I do? On top of it all, I had to tell my 9-year-old son that we were not going to the zoo. I did not want to fail him! How do I explain it to him without making him doubt God in the future? Was there a job that I was supposed to be doing? I was at the end of my rope.

It was my custom to go by the post office to check the ministry mail on my way home. When I checked that day, I found a personal check for $90 from a friend. That would sound like good news, but it was 12:30 PM on a Saturday, and the banks were closed. Because I had obeyed God and gone to school, now I would not be able to cash it! Should I have called in sick? I had 100% attendance, but was that pride? The thoughts were almost too much for me, so I prayed again, saying, *"Jesus, please help me! I feel like I am looking at a dead end!"* My check register said that I had 86 cents in the bank. Then I had an idea. If I deposited the check in the bank ATM, it would not be available until Monday. Maybe something had not cleared, and I could get $5 for gas even though I could not imagine how any check would still be outstanding since my last deposit two weeks ago.

I went to the ATM and checked my balance before making my deposit. When I read the tiny slip of paper from the machine, I thought I must be hallucinating! I rubbed my eyes and looked at it twice to be sure and almost went to a passerby to ask him to read it to me! Before depositing the $90 check, the ATM said I had $75.86 in the bank! I felt dizzy! I had asked God for $75 by 1 PM on Saturday. Here it was Saturday at 12:50 PM, and I had $75 in my bank account. Plus, I had a check for $90 yet to deposit! I deposited the check and withdrew $75. At the first gasoline station, I filled up the car, which took two gallons less than the capacity listed in the owner's manual, meaning there were still two gallons in it! That is completely impossible! It was empty when I put in the eight gallons on Monday, and then I drove over 300 miles! How could a car that gets 18 miles per gallon go over 300 miles on six gallons of gasoline and over 155 miles were driven after the gas needle registered "E"? God multiplied the gas in my car! It was a miracle!

After suffering through my week-long tribulation, something strange happened to me when I received that money in the nick of time. The Bible says:

> ...we glory in tribulations also: knowing that tribulation worketh patience; And patience, experience; and experience, hope: And hope maketh not ashamed; because the love of God is shed abroad in our hearts by the Holy Ghost which is given unto us (Romans 5:3-5).

I felt the exhilaration of answered prayer along with the release of the emotional pressure. Then suddenly, bubbling up out of my midsection, I felt a love that was different from anything I had ever experienced. It was a supernatural love for our merciful God who dealt with my anxiety and pain by giving me a miracle, and that love was being poured out on me by the Holy Spirit. That experience turned out to be the doorway for me into the world of God's miracles.

Throughout the years, that experience has been repeated time and again, so much in fact that it has become the norm. However, now instead of being small amounts of money that I need, it can be thousands, but He does it anyway, without my ability being involved. I have never had the money or the ability to provide for my family's needs and the ministry. It has always been impossible for me, but God has done it anyway, serving as a constant reminder of the reality of the Living God. The timing of the supply, the exact amount needed coming in the nick of time, mixed with the feeling of relief, is proof of the Living God.

One time I related this testimony to an atheist, and in true atheistic fashion, he said abruptly, *"I don't believe in your invisible friend!"* I laughed and said:

> *"Well, brother, someone has been talking to me for almost all of my life. He has done miracles. He has healed my body and taken care of my family and me. On that occasion, I hadn't told anyone about my need, and someone answered my prayer and gave me exactly what I had requested just in the nick of time! I asked Him who He was, and He said His Name is Jesus, but if it's not Him! WHO IS IT?"*

15

THE ARMY OF THE LORD

> The centurion answered and said, Lord, I am not worthy that thou shouldest come under my roof: but speak the word only, and my servant shall be healed. For I am a man under authority, having soldiers under me: and I say to this man, Go, and he goeth; and to another, Come, and he cometh; and to my servant, Do this, and he doeth it. When Jesus heard it, he marveled, and said to them that followed, Verily I say unto you, I have not found so great faith, no, not in Israel (Matthew 8:8-10).

What is the Church? It is not a building, nor is it a social club or a fraternal organization. If we attempt to describe the Church from the standpoint of the New Testament, it would be more accurate to say that the Church is an army: a spiritual paramilitary organization fighting a spiritual war against unseen adversaries. It is the living, breathing body of the Messiah here on the earth.

Similar to the centurion's relationship to Caesar, I am an officer in the army of the Lord, and I answer to the Holy Spirit and those whom He sends. At a church or on the road, I maintain the spiritual position of "attention," and at home, I am at "parade rest," attempting to be in a state of listening for His voice constantly. I am under orders!

Relationships always empower ministry, and an experience with the military helps to understand how the ministry and faith work. Faith can easily be comprehended by thinking of it this way: It does what the Bible says while having a relationship with God through the Holy Spirit. We must do what He says, regardless of how we feel about it. Success in the ministry can be easier if the principle of being under orders is understood.

Faith is obeying the orders of our superior, whether God or someone He has sent. We simply cannot obey God without a good attitude toward the people we serve. We live as God says to live, and we do what God says to do. I love the church, and I love being there, but I do not attend a church because I like something about that ministry. I do not stay in a particular church because they treat me well or because I like their children's ministry or worship service. I never leave a church because I do not get my way or I get offended. God assigns me a job to do, and I am there simply because it is my post. I cannot leave until headquarters or the commanding officer determines that my time there is finished, and then I am sent to another duty station.

The military was created for war. As in any war, wherever I am assigned is usually complete with spiritual violence and many problems. However, as a faithful officer, I cannot be the one with the problem. If there are difficulties in the performance of my duty, the word from God is always the same, *"Mark, be scriptural; do whatever is necessary and stay on target!"* Our performance in completing our assigned tasks in this military is never based on good or bad treatment by those around us. We must remember that we are involved in a love war, so sometimes we may feel mistreated or used. Obeying orders is difficult at times, but promotion always accompanies completion.

If we study the Bible for ourselves and obey what is written, avoid sin, and have a strong prayer life, we will continue in a place where God will oversee both the ones in authority and us. Only God is the infallible supreme commander. From time to time, a good leader will always state that fact in one way or another and encourage people to seek God and to obey Him above all others. Many are concerned about being deceived by the pastor, but in the local church, deception from the pulpit is not as common as some would have us believe. But in the rare cases in which it does happen, it is usually the result of people not using common sense, not reading and doing the Bible for themselves, not paying attention to the things that go on around them, and ignoring the Holy Spirit.

16

GETTING YOUR HOUSE IN ORDER

I am sure it is common among honest people, but what I thought I would do in life was much different than what God planned for me.

When I left the forest and went to Bible school in 1983, I had many ideas about what Jesus wanted to do with me. I thought I would finish school, return to the forest, and start a church or help a pastor friend grow his church. But, through the years, God has taught me a great deal about making plans. Many times, my plans were not His plans. I think that is why Pastor Osteen always said to *"travel light and hang loose."* The world teaches, *"Plan your work and work your plan,"* but on the mission field, the saying should be, *"Plan your work and change your plan."* We must learn to be flexible because our way is not the only way, and we would probably be surprised to find out that our way is not necessarily the right way!

The following thought always overshadowed teachings in Bible school and language school:

> *"Open your heart and prepare for a change. You have your plans, but let God have his way. The United States has less than 5% of the world's population but has 95% of the ministers of the gospel! Allow God to have control of your thoughts and open yourself to new possibilities. Nothing in the New Testament is beyond your reach."*

After receiving God's direction to learn Spanish, I began to pray about the country God wanted me to go to, and He said, *"Peru."*

When I went to language school, I thought I would go to Peru following graduation in 1985. As the time for graduation from Kingsway drew near, I had a vivid dream one night. In it, a Peruvian man stood in the parking lot and said, *"Wait! You aren't coming to Peru for four more years."* In the dream, I asked, *"Four years? Why?"* He said, *"Because the roads are not yet ready. You have things that you must do first."* When I woke up, I asked the Lord the meaning, and He said, *"Things in your family are yet undone, and you have to raise support and do more preparation. So, take heart, you most certainly are going, but not until 1988."*

God gave us families, and because He is the source of family ties, He understands our desire for them to be saved. So, as we find out His Will for our lives and follow Him in obedience, He has a way of continuing to minister and help us get our houses in order.

17

PAPA'S CONVERSION

Papa was my maternal grandfather. Walter was my stepfather, and Woody was my father. They were good men but very tough. They belonged to the World War II generation and possessed a different kind of mind and work ethic than what we have become accustomed to in the 21st Century. I loved all three men and had a burden for them, often praying for their salvation. I warned them about hell but to no avail. In my prayers for them, I would say to the Lord, *"God, how could I ever truly enjoy heaven if the men that raised me are in hell? Please do something."*

My desire for their salvation was a "pie in the sky" dream for which I prayed but did not hold much hope. I knew that it would take a direct intervention of God for it to happen. All three could not trust anyone other than themselves. Even though they loved their families and were good-hearted for the most part, the few times I attempted to witness to them were *not* fruitful and *very* unpleasant.

It was my custom to sit on the porch and listen to Papa tell me stories of his youth. It was fascinating to hear about a time long past in a world I could only imagine.

He was born in 1910 in Houston, Texas, and shortly after his birth, his parents returned to Alia, Sicily. They were Sicilian-born and did not stay in the United States. Papa's parents did not speak English, and his mother, Silvia, was a Sephardic Jew and a member of the European diaspora. Later in life, when I asked why no one had ever told me that I was Jewish, they just said, *"We learned to not talk about that."*

In Sicily, Papa was raised during the time of Benito Mussolini and his Italian Nationalist Fascist Party. In elementary school at twelve years of age, Papa was removed from his 6*th* grade class, taken to the principal's office, where they sat him down and said, *"Giuseppe, you have too much education. We are taking you to the cobbler, and you will learn how to make shoes so that you can take care of yourself."* So, he lived and ate at the shoe shop, worked for the cobbler for six years until he was 18; at that time, he was given a guitar and sent on his way. Papa used to say that the cobbler did not pay him because he was learning a trade, which was more valuable than money.

During his time with the cobbler, he studied Marxism and claimed to be an atheist. When I was a teenager and asked him about God, he said, *"I don't believe in any god, and you believe because you don't want to work!"* In 1928, after he finished his apprenticeship with the cobbler, he joined Mussolini's Blackshirt Army. As he stood in line to jump through the ring-of-fire making him a full member of the Italian version of the dreaded "Nazi SS," his father, Franco, ran up to him and pulled him out of line. He slapped his son across the face and shook his finger at him, and said, *"Shame on you! I am sending you to your country!"* They put him on a boat bound for New York and from there he went to Kansas City, Missouri, where he worked as a shoemaker. In 1930, Papa married my grandmother, Louise, and they moved to Houston soon after.

My grandparents had three daughters, and I was the first-born male to my grandfather's family, so he wanted to take an active role in my life. In the 1970s and 80s, Papa enjoyed going to Lakewood, where I would often see him sitting there with a big smile. At the time, his goal for my life was for me to be a doctor or a lawyer, so I could make him proud. When I decided to follow Jesus into the ministry, it made him angry. Papa fought with me for the first four years of my ministry, and I grew to dread my visits with him because of what he would say. I continued to pray and refused to give up, even in the face of sometimes physical resistance to my decision.

Around the time of my graduation from language school, I visited my grandparents' home. As I was getting ready to return to South Texas to continue my ministry, Papa, who was 75 years old at the time, asked to talk to me. I shuddered and prayed, *"Father, here we go again! What am I supposed to say to him?"* The Lord said, *"Say what Caleb said, 'As for me and my house, we will serve the Lord.'"*

I went into his breakfast room, and my grandmother was in the kitchen. Papa was sitting at a round glass table, not looking happy. I stood in front of him, but I said:

> *"Papa, before you say anything, I have to tell you something. I respect you. You are a hard worker and have accomplished wonderful things in your life against odds that I can never understand. But sir, with great admiration, I have to tell you that there is nothing that you can do or say to change my mind about Jesus, because 'as for me and my house, we will serve the Lord.'"*

It was not like him, but Papa remained quiet for a little while; a tear ran down his face, and he said, *"I want to do that too, my boy! I don't want to go to hell."* My grandmother must have overheard the conversation because she dropped a metal tray in the kitchen. I could not believe my ears; it was a miracle. I went over and sat down in a chair beside him. I took his hand that was calloused from years of hard work, and I said, *"Papa, please pray with me."* I led him in the sinner's prayer, and when we finished, with tears running down his face, he jumped to his feet and said over and over, *"Sweet Jesus, thank You. Thank You!"* He said to my grandmother, *"Baby, give me my checkbook!"* and wrote a check to the ministry for $300. He became our treasurer and staunchly supported my ministry until his death. He was my premier advocate.

In 1994 when he was 84, Papa got sick and was taken to the hospital in Huntsville, Texas. One morning in

February, the family was called to the hospital because Papa had passed away in the night. The nurses left him as they found him until the family arrived. When everyone went into his room, there he was, lying in bed with a huge smile frozen on his face. I told everyone, *"That was Papa's gift to us. He and Jesus are telling us that he's safe. He probably saw all of our dearly departed friends and family and smiled as he left his body behind."*

My grandmother Louise lived for Papa. They were married for 64 years. When he died, she immediately began to fade, and two years later, she passed away. I was pastoring a church in Miami, Florida, and in February of 1996, I got the last $300 check from my grandparents in her handwriting. She wrote it from the hospital in College Station, Texas, and her writing was very shaky as if she were struggling to write it. The money was a kind thing they did for me that showed their commitment to Jesus and what He had done in my life. I called her to thank her, but she was unable to talk except to say, *"That's OK!"*

A cousin sat with her in the hospital every day that she was there. A few days after making that last phone call, my cousin called me and told me that my grandmother had gone to heaven and wanted to tell me the story of her passing. She said my grandmother went into a coma a short while after I called to thank her for the check. For three or four days, she struggled to breathe because her lungs were filling with fluid, and the doctors said that her death was imminent. My cousin said:

> *"I was sitting by her bedside, and suddenly the gurgling stopped. She began to breathe normally and sat up straight in the bed. Her face was bright, and she was looking toward the foot of the bed in delight. In a clear and perfectly normal voice, she said 'There's Papa!' I said, 'Where is he?', and she said, 'He's at the foot of the bed, and he's with the Master!' I didn't know what to say, so I said, 'I think they've come for you.'"*

My grandmother immediately laid back down and left with Jesus and Papa.

18

WALTER'S WEEKEND

Walter was my stepfather, and he and my mother had moved from Houston to Denver, Colorado, in the late 1970s. When they heard I was graduating from language school and going to Peru, they decided that they would come to my graduation. I was surprised to hear that Walter was coming because he never showed much interest in the things of God, even though I could remember once or twice in the past when I would see tears in his eyes while watching a Jesus movie or sitting in a church at Easter.

During language school, I lived in a 17-foot travel trailer by some orange trees on a farm in South Texas. On May 24, 1985, I was in the trailer, praying about Walter's visit. I did not know what to say or how to pray, so I prayed in other tongues. While praying, suddenly, the Lord said in that familiar voice that emanated from my midsection, *"This is Walter's weekend."*

Walter was a 6'2" graduate of Texas A&M in College Station, Texas. He was a U.S. Air Force Reserve Officer who was promoted to Major upon his discharge. He was a loving man but tough, complete with a federal firearms dealer's license and an airplane, and Walter knew cuss words for every occasion. I had tried witnessing to him once before with negative results and did not look forward to making another vain attempt. So I said, *"God, if this is Walter's weekend, that's fine with me, but I am going to leave that to You because I tried before, and it didn't work!"*

Later that evening, I went by the McAllen International Airport and picked up Walter and my mother to take them to the hotel where they would be staying. As was Walter's custom, after we got to the hotel, he said, *"Let's go for a ride."* So we drove around the area and went over to Reynosa, Mexico to see the sights.

During our two days visiting, Walter asked, "*Son, what are you doing for a living?*" I told him I was working for a church and doing just about anything else I could find to do. Then, in his "colorful" way, he said, *"I have been a Christian all my life."* I did not know what approach to take, but since God had spoken to me about it being his weekend, I said, *"Walter, you are and always have been a better man than I am. You are a good provider, and you have always worked hard. I owe you a debt that I could never pay, but I don't think you're a Christian."* He said, *"Oh yeah? Why do you think that, son?"* I said, *"Walter, with much respect, I have to tell you that the first thing that cleans up when someone gets saved is the mouth, and you have a cussing problem."* He looked kind of surprised and then changed the subject.

On Sunday evening, May 26th, he attended my graduation, and we went out to eat and back to their hotel afterward. They planned to leave early the next morning to drive the 350 miles to Houston to visit family, and I also needed to get up early. I had been waiting all weekend for something to happen with no results, so at 9 PM, I thought to myself, *"It's now or never."* I leaned on the dresser; Walter sat on the edge of the bed, and my mother sat on the other side of the room. Suddenly, it got very quiet. There was no road noise, no air conditioners running, and not a sound of any kind. I could tell that God was working with me, so in fear and trembling, I said very quietly, *"Walter, I think that Jesus wants you to give Him your heart."*

After about 10 seconds, he began to shake, and he trembled so violently that he slid off the bed to the floor onto his knees, and he began to cry out loud and said, *"Jesus! Have mercy on me! I don't want to go to hell! I want to go to heaven! Save me, Lord! I repent for my sins!"* He did not stay in the floor long because the Lord Jesus heard him, and Walter jumped to his feet, clapped his hands, and shouted over and over, *"Hallelujah! I'm saved! Thank you, Jesus! Bless God!"* He looked at me with a huge smile and said, *"Thank you, son."* I told him that He owed me nothing. In less than a minute, he changed so much that it shocked us all, and from that moment on, his cussing stopped; he used his tongue to bless God for the rest of his life.

19

MOTHER'S DIVINE DELIVERANCE

Walter and my mother eventually returned to Denver, where Walter sold his guns, airplane, house, and company, and they went to Rhema Bible Training Center in Tulsa, Oklahoma.

As I mentioned earlier, my relationship with my mother was complicated. I never understood why or what I had done, but it always seemed like something was wrong, and she could not explain it. I used to wonder what it would be like to have a smiling mother who baked cakes and pies and was always happy with me. Even though I lived with my mother until I was 16, had it not been for my grandmother, I probably would never have known what it was like to have a mother.

On December 2, 1993, my mother was in Texas, and Walter had come to Peru to help us move back to Texas. I woke up that morning, and the second my eyes opened,

I heard the audible voice of the Lord say, *"Your mother is coming back to you, but she's coming back with a debt to pay."* This time, the voice did not emanate from my midsection, but it seemed like someone was in the room with me. I got up and went into the living room where Walter was having coffee and asked him, *"Where is mother going?"* and told him about the voice. He had no idea of her schedule because she was in Texas but thought maybe she was going on a trip of some kind. So, we called her on the phone, and she was well but did not know where she was going next either.

A week later on December 9*th*, we left to fly back to Miami to catch a flight for Texas. A pastor friend was to pick us up when we landed in Houston at 2 AM. We called my mother from a public pay phone upon our arrival in Miami, but she did not answer. Since we were pressed for time, we boarded a plane for Memphis, where we would catch the last leg to Houston.

When we disembarked in Memphis, we called my mother, and my grandmother answered and was sobbing and saying:

> *"She's dead! She's dead! We came home from the store and found her lying on the floor with her eyes open and not breathing. We couldn't wake her, so we called the paramedics. She had been lying there so long without breathing, but they got her breathing again. They are taking her to the hospital in Conroe, Texas!"*

We could not talk further because we had to board the plane. I had to hang up.

At 2 AM, we arrived in Houston, and a friend picked us up and drove us to Conroe. Walter was noticeably hurting, and I told him, *"Walter, I don't know what is going on, but we can see why the Lord said that she is coming back to us! So, don't worry; we'll just believe and see what will happen."*

We arrived at the hospital around 4 AM and went into the emergency room; she was lying on a table with her eyes open and a machine breathing for her. My grandmother was in the room, weeping almost uncontrollably.

The nurses informed us that the doctor had waited for us and escorted us into a small room with a lighted screen. After 10 minutes, the doctor came with some x-rays they had taken of her brain. He said that she had a massive stroke and showed us the shadows on the x-ray that indicated there was blood on her brain. As a result, they had taken a brain scan, and the doctor said that because she quit breathing for so long, the brain scan showed no activity; she was brain-dead, and it was impossible for her ever to recover. He said, *"We have kept her alive so you could arrive and say goodbye to her, but with your permission, we are going to disconnect the machine."* He continued:

> *"I heard that you are ministers of the gospel, and I am very sorry, but if you are going to pray, please pray that she passes away when we unplug the machine. If she*

> *survives, she will be a vegetable in a nursing home in need of constant care until she finally dies."*

Walter began to cry, and I laughed. I shocked myself, but after traveling all day and half the night, I did not have the energy to wonder why. My response to the doctor was:

> *"One week ago today, I heard the audible voice of God, and He said that she was coming back to us with a debt to pay. We thought He meant that she was going on a vacation or a mission trip but would eventually come back. Now we can see what He meant."*

The doctor was a very kind believer, and he said, *"That's what you need! You need God Himself to do something because we can do nothing for her."* So we went ahead and gave our permission for him to take her off life support after I talked to my grandmother. I could not explain why I was laughing; I was not happy. I did not think it was funny, but I laughed! It was not until weeks later that I understood why I had that reaction.

I went back into the emergency room where my grandmother was crying uncontrollably next to my mother's body. One nurse had her arm around my grandmother, and the other nurse was with my mother on the other side of the bed. There were patients in other parts of the room with tears in their eyes out of compassion for us. I told the nurses, *"God says that she is coming back,"* but they did not seem to be able to believe it. I went to my mother, put my hand on her head, leaned down about a foot from her face, looked in her lifeless eyes, and said:

> *"A week ago in Lima, Jesus said that you're coming back to us. The Bible says that believers will lay hands on the sick, and they will recover. Brain—I'm not talking about you. I'm talking to you; you be healed in the Name of Jesus of Nazareth! Life—come back in Jesus' Name!"*

There was no response or change, and she was still lying there with her eyes open and no movement, except the machine breathing for her. I went over and carefully took my grandmother by the hand and into the waiting room. I told her:

> *"Mother's not dead. She's inside her body, and she can see and hear you making a fuss and cannot respond. Imagine how you would feel if you saw your family acting like that and couldn't say anything to them to make them feel better."*

My grandmother said, *"Why are you happy? How could you be so cold? That is my daughter and your mother, and she's dead! How could you be laughing?"* I sternly said:

> *"She's not dead! Before any of this happened, God told me over a week ago that she is coming back, so that is what I*

> *believe! I don't know why I'm laughing, but it is going to happen. I don't know how, but she's going to live! Now, Papa is at the house. He's 83 and needs you. You have been up here all day, and you are 77. I don't want you to make yourself sick. So, we are going to go back in the room, and you are going to tell her that you will see her later and then go home and go to bed, but please, no crying and making a fuss. You are breaking her heart!"*

My grandmother promised that she would behave if she could, so we returned to the emergency room. The first thing I saw was another patient with one hand over her mouth and pointing with the other hand in the direction of my mother. As we came around the corner, we saw a nurse flat up against the wall with her eyes wide open in shock. My mother was sitting on the side of the bed, crying as she tried to pull out the breathing tube from her mouth! I stopped her from pulling the tube and said, *"Mother, glad to see you're back! Let the doctor come in here and help you!"* I kept on laughing, and my grandmother stopped crying! Walter came in and shouted, *"Hallelujah!"* The terrified nurse ran down the hall to get the doctor. The patient that was pointing relayed what had happened, *"After you and your grandmother left, your mom began to move and shake, then she sat up! When she came back to life, the nurse backed up against the wall! We didn't know what was going on!"*

About that time, the nurse came running in with some other nurses and the doctor. The doctor said, *"Obviously, it wasn't as bad as we thought, but she will never speak again because this killed the speech center of her brain."* We all just laughed. They admitted her to the hospital, and the next morning when I walked into the room to see her, she said, *"Good morning, son!"* Jesus had done another mighty miracle.

As one professor at Bible school used to say, *"God is the only person in the Universe who can do what He jolly-well pleases. The rest of us are limited in our abilities."* The fact is that God can and will do what He pleases whether our doctrine agrees with Him or not. So, after the incident with my mother and another similar incident in Peru, I studied raising the dead in the New Testament. I am aware that in certain apostolic works, raising the dead is quite common, and it is true that Jesus commissioned the 70 who were sent out two-by-two to raise the dead. Yet, raising the dead is not something we can typically do because it was not included in the Great Commission; it was something He told the 70 to do, but not the church. In Matthew 28, Mark 16, and Acts 1, when Jesus commissioned the church, He never said to raise the dead, but He did say to lay hands on the sick and they will recover. Therefore, in most cases, raising the dead must be as He wills, for His purposes.

When God's church raises the dead, in 99.9% of the cases, you must have four manifestations of the Holy Spirit operating at the same time or near the same time:

First, it must begin with a word of wisdom, or Him telling you to do it or not to do it. A word of wisdom is supernatural knowledge about the will of God or a future event. In other words, we must know that is what God wants to do in advance for that particular person. **Then,** a gift of special faith must come, knowing without a doubt that the prayer is going to be answered. **Next,** there must be a working of miracles to bring the person back from the other side. **Finally,** there must be a gift of healing, else whatever killed the person in the first place will kill them again.

In my mother's case, when God spoke and said that she was going to come back, that was the word of wisdom. I was unexplainably laughing because I was certain that it would happen since God had said it would, which was the gift of special faith. God did a miracle and brought her back, and then the healing took place.

My mother lived a normal life for another five years, and she was a real mother to me. Her personality was different, and she was so happy. It was a pleasure spending those years with her, as she and Walter helped me in the ministry in Florida.

In 1998, I was sitting next to the bed, holding Walter's hand the day before he passed away. He kept looking toward the door and saying, *"Hey, who are you guys? What are you doing in here? Get out of here!"* The nurses kept saying he was delirious. After the nurses left, I leaned over and said quietly, *"Walter, who are you talking to?"* He said, *"Those men over there! Don't you see them? There are two of them wearing long white robes, waving incense burners in the air. I don't want them here, but they won't leave!"* Through tears, I said, *"Walter, I don't want you to leave, but it looks to me like the angels are preparing the way for you."* He squeezed my hand and said, *"Son, there are only two things in this world that are worth anything at all, and they are what we have done for Jesus and the loving relationships we have shared."* That evening he passed away, and 12 days later, my mother joined him in heaven.

Deliverance is a process. From time to time, no matter how hard I tried to suppress them, the memories of my childhood seemed to haunt me. Eight years after my mother's death, I went to sleep thinking about certain things that happened, and I had a vivid dream:

I was in a beautiful, wooded area. Flowers were blooming everywhere, and the trees were a surreal green. The smell of springtime in the air was intoxicating and made me feel like sitting down at one of the round cement picnic tables to bask in the sunshine. To my right, there was a 10-foot tall chain-link fence with barbwire on top to keep anyone from crossing over, and there was a gate in the fence with a padlock on it. Through the fence, I could see a forest, and in the distance, I could make out beautiful homes on the other side. There appeared to be a long line of people coming our way along a path, where they began to line up in front of the locked gate.

In the dream, I had no idea what I was doing there, but I knew it was a dream. Suddenly, the gardener came and unlocked the gate; he opened it, and the lines of people flowed into where I was. I sat there watching people that I did not know come through the gate, and suddenly in the crowd, there was a face that I recognized. It was my mother! My mouth dropped open as I got up and went to her, saying, *"Mother! This is incredible! What are you doing here? You're dead!"* She appeared to be in her 30s with a beautiful smile; she took me by my right hand and, without a word, led me back to the round picnic table and sat down across from me. In the dream, I could not get over it. From across the table, I kept staring at her, and she wasn't speaking, so I said, *"You have the face of an angel!"* She gave me an even bigger smile and crossed her eyes like she used to do when I was a child. I said, *"OK, then you have the face of a crazy angel!"* There was a man at a table next to me, and I elbowed him and said, *"That's my mother! She's dead and is going to disappear any minute because this is a dream, and she's a ghost."* Immediately her smile evaporated, and she began to cry with a look of deep hurt on her face. Through her tears, she said, *"Mark, I am so tired of being a ghost in your life! Please live! I want you to live"* I began to cry along with her, and I said, *"Of course, I will! I'll live!"* She got up, took me by the hand, and we walked back to the gate. She hugged me and walked back to the other side and down the path; the gardener came and locked the gate.

Then, I woke up.

20

MY FATHER'S JOURNEY

My father's name was Woody. I did not know him as well as I would have liked, but he was a kind soul and a deep thinker. He was a former member of the Mensa Society of America with a very high IQ. He worked for a large computer firm in Washington, DC, carried the civilian rank of Navy Commander, and programmed computers for the U.S. Navy, helping calculate orbits for satellites.

When my daddy was a young man, he was spiritually wounded by a church in Houston and had never quite gotten over it. He left the church, studied Buddhism, and claimed to be an agnostic. Early in my Christian life, I tried to talk to him about Jesus, and he said, *"Are you witnessing to me?"* I admitted that I was, and he said, *"Never speak to me about that again."* I said simply, *"Yes, sir."*

During my time of preparation to go to Peru, I felt that I should visit him at his home in rural Virginia. As my son, Jason, and I drove to Virginia for our visit, I shared with him that we were going because the Bible says I should honor my father. However, we were not going to talk to him about Jesus because he had forbidden me. I explained that if Jesus wanted something to happen, it would be up to Him.

We arrived at my father's home in the beautiful Shenandoah hills of north-central Virginia, and we visited for a few days without mentioning Jesus. During the visit, he asked me what I did for a living, and I vaguely answered, *"Oh, odds and ends. I'm sure you don't want to talk about it."*

The day before we left to go back to Texas, we toured the Smithsonian museums in Washington DC. On the way back, I noticed the anointing was on me in a powerful way. I felt lightheaded and had a feeling inside that I get before a miracle happens. I asked Jason if he was feeling well, and he was, so I could not put my finger on what was going on.

When we returned to my daddy's home after our long day, we were sitting in his living room, and he abruptly said:

> *"I dreamed last night that I was talking in a strange language. It consisted of a lot of Z's and Th's and sounded Aramaic. I had no idea what I was saying, but the more I spoke in that language, the better I felt. It*

> *filled me with so much peace, and I wouldn't say anything to you about it. However, just before I woke up from the dream, I said, 'I have to talk to Mark about this in the morning.' Do you have any idea why I would want to talk to you about it?"*

I said, *"That sure explains the anointing I have been under for so long today. I believe I can help you with your dream, but I am going to have to talk to you about Jesus to do it, and you told me not to talk to you about Him."* So, he said, *"It was my dream, and I'm asking you about it. What does it mean?"*

I went and got my Bible and opened to 1 Corinthians and showed him where Paul the apostle talked about speaking in tongues. Then, I explained the difference between the gift of tongues and a personal prayer language. My daddy's friend was sitting on the other sofa. I had met her during our visit, but I knew almost nothing about her. Then, with no warning, in the middle of my explanation of tongues, the woman on the other sofa threw both hands in the air and began to shout in other tongues! I was startled because we were speaking quietly, and my daddy said, *"That's the language I was speaking in my dream!"*

I said, *"Daddy, why don't you forgive that church in Houston that wounded you? Then ask Jesus to forgive you for leaving Him and to take you back!"* He said he would like to do that, so I led him in a prayer of forgiveness and repentance. Then, I led him in a prayer, asking God to give him the Holy Ghost, and I placed my hand on his head, saying, *"Father, baptize him in the Holy Ghost!"* My daddy said, *"Excuse me a moment."* He got up, went into the bathroom, and said, *"It happened to me! It happened to me! It's like I found what I have been looking for all my life, and it was right here on the tip of my tongue!"*

When we were leaving to go back to Texas, daddy asked for my newsletter, and I began to send it to him. We enjoyed a more father and son relationship in the few years he had left. He even supported my ministry from time to time!

During the summer of 1998, I was on the telephone with my daddy every evening of the month before he died. It was so enriching to find out about the ins and outs of his personality because it helped me learn about myself. About six weeks before my stepfather Walter passed away, my daddy went to heaven. The day before he died, I called him and said, *"Daddy, how are you? Is it OK with you and Jesus?"* He said, *"I'm fine, son."* Those were the last words he spoke to me on this planet.

It was a traumatic time for me with those three family deaths and funerals that I performed in a short time. In less than eight weeks, both parents and my stepfather parted this world bound for heaven. My mother was the last to depart, and a week following her passing, I had a vivid dream:

I was in a place that was pitch black where I could not see anything. Reaching out in the darkness, I felt a wall to my back and front. There was open space to my left, so I put my hands on the front wall and carefully felt my way along, trying to get out of that tight space. After side-stepping 20 feet or so, I came to a corner where the front and back walls turned 90 degrees to the left. I could see to the left that the wall in front was part of a vast building, and there was a window in the wall, with light shining out of it. I side-stepped toward the window, cupped my hands, and looked inside. It was a massive church with pews going off into the distance. The walls were endless, and I could see no ceiling.

The air inside was filled with the smoke of the glory of God. I said, *"This must be the heavenly tabernacle in New Jerusalem!"* I did not see many people, but a few rows up from where I was looking, sitting together on the pew, were my grandmother, parents, stepfather, Cherokee Uncle, Little Ma'am, and several others, all staring at the front. I remember the look on Walter's face as he stared toward the front. He had a look on his face of satisfaction that showed he had found the goal of his life's ambitions. In the dream, I was astounded as my grandmother turned and looked at me and waved as if to say, *"We will see you soon!"*

21

MISSION TO PERU

During the following four years after 1985, in addition to the breakthroughs in my family, I worked as an associate pastor at two different churches: one in English and the other in Spanish. I also served as a traveling evangelist in the United States and Mexico, spending my time meeting new friends, raising support, and working on improving my Spanish.

In 1988, God finally allowed me to go on a three-week trip to Peru for the first time to "spy out the land." I had a friend who lived in Lima, and we were going to stay with him while there. If you feel God has called you to go someplace for Him and you hate the place, there's a chance that God did not give you the grace to be there.

On the night before leaving, I dreamt I was in Peru, and I was digging a deep hole in fertile ground. After the hole was finished, I carefully took a bundle of mimosa tree roots from my yard in the forest and planted them in Peru. Then in the dream, God "showed" me that I was to work for my friend's pastor and said that the relationship would last a lifetime.

When I arrived in Lima, I loved it! I had never encountered a friendlier bunch of people or a more accepting society! I asked my friend about his pastor, and I made an appointment to meet him. I shared the dream with him and how I thought God had called me to help him. He and his wife oversaw a church that had begun just four years earlier with only eight people, but in 1988 had 700 in attendance, and it was growing fast. He told me that they would pray, and if I returned the following year, I would be welcome.

I had prayed for four years before I moved to Peru. In prayer, I determined we needed $10,000 in cash and $1800 per month in support. I traveled almost coast to coast throughout the U.S. and Mexico during those four years. I met pastors and individuals, and if someone said, *"If we can ever do anything for you, please let us know,"* I would say, *"As a matter of fact, we are raising monthly support...."* I preached in churches. I asked for referrals. I wrote letters and made telephone calls since the time to leave was coming up soon. Just a month before we were to go, I had the airline tickets, but only $4500 in cash and $1300 per month in support. I felt pressured due to the unknown.

The questions that flooded my mind were always the same: Did I do enough? Should I forget this and go to work somewhere? There is one of the worst terrorist organizations in the world in Peru; is God trying to tell me not to take my family there? So, I asked the Lord in prayer, *"God, I have needs, and the current supply is much less than I requested. Am I doing the right thing?"* He said, *"Yes, you are doing what I told you to do! By My Spirit, it will be enough! Are you going to believe Me or your bank balance?"* I said to myself, *"I was afraid He would say that,"* but to Him, I said, *"Yes, Lord."* So it was settled in my heart once and for all.

The return airline tickets from Lima had an open date for the return flight. At that time, I could call the airlines in Peru, and with a 24-hour notice, they would find seats for us to return, but I could not get a refund, and they cost us $1500! The day before we were to leave, I was driving through Huntsville, Texas around 1 PM, and I had to get up at 3:00 the following morning for the flight to Miami and on to Peru. I turned on the radio, and the Christian music was interrupted by a news report saying, *"The U.S. Embassy is requesting all Americans to avoid Lima, Peru. The British Embassy was bombed, and there is reported street fighting."* This surprise was something that I was not expecting, I went home and tried to call my friend in Peru, and there was no answer! He always answered! Why was this happening, and now?! I got on my knees and *said, "Jesus, You told me to do this. The date is something that You spoke to me a year ago. What do I do now?"* He simply said, *"Go!"*

The plane arrived in Miami the next day, and before they allowed us to board the flight to Lima, they took us to a classroom to give us a "class" on terrorism and a stern warning. We had to sign papers saying that we had been warned, and we were going against the advice of the U.S. Government.

We finally arrived in Lima. When my Peruvian friend picked us up at the airport, I asked him about bombings and street fighting. His response was, "*Wow! That sounds frightening! Where is that going on?*" I said the radio said it was going on here in Lima, and they made us sign papers at the airport in Miami saying that we knew that coming here was too dangerous. He said, "*No kidding! About a month ago, I heard there was a car bomb at the British Embassy, but street fighting...? I don't know anything about that.*" He said, "*There always seems to be something going on, though, and it can be a bit violent from time to time.*" I asked him how long the violence had been going on, and he said, "*Since the 1820s. That's why God has sent you here to be a missionary!*" We had a good laugh over that.

For the first couple of days in Lima, we stayed at my friend's small home down by the "Salto del Frei," the beautiful cliffs in Miraflores, overlooking the Pacific Ocean with a pebble beach several hundred feet below. I asked my friend if he knew of anyone who wanted to rent an apartment or a home, and he took me to a realtor's office. The realtor asked me how much I wanted to spend, and I told her that I wanted to spend as little as possible but be in a good neighborhood.

The realtor knew of a house in "El Rosedal" that was renting for $400 per month and drove us over to look at it. It was a furnished 5000 square foot home in a gated community, with mahogany fixtures and huge jade plants growing in an indoor garden under the staircase, complete with a telephone! I gave the owner $400 for the first month's rent and a $400 deposit. We bought kitchen accessories, a microwave, a television and food, and we were ready to go! I had $2500 in cash remaining. When people found out that I was actually in Peru, the monthly support started coming to the tune of $2000 per month—exceeding the amount I had calculated.

Other than with the Marines, I had never gone to another continent. I had also never been a full-time missionary, so I had many ideas about what being a missionary would include, what I would teach, where I would go, and what I would do. When I arrived, I worked hard and served the pastor. I saw and participated in so many amazing miracles; I would have to write another book just to talk about them. However, the biggest work was not done through me; it was done in me.

The pastor took me to his office, we spoke in Spanish, and I asked him what he wanted me to do. He replied by saying that he wanted me to obey God on a day-to-day basis, and then he told me part of God's expectations for me. He said, *"God asked me a question recently, and I want to ask you the same question: Do you like the people?"* He told me when God asked him that same question, he responded, *"Father, I love the people."* He said God showed him that loving them was something that he did as a Christian, but as a man, he must learn to like them—their music, food, homes, and whatever made them who they are. He continued by saying, *"That may sound strange, but it is a key to being successful with any people."* I told him that I would try my best. In my quest to not just love the people, I found out what being a true missionary is all about as *I became a Peruvian.*

Jesus of Nazareth was 100 percent man and 100 percent God. The human part of Him was the first missionary, and He is proof that to minister to a nation or group of people, the missionary must be able to understand life from their point of view. The mission field changed me, and that was the biggest work that was accomplished.

Lima is a huge city on the west coast of Peru. It is tropical, but the temperatures are more temperate due to the cold water from the Humboldt current just off the coast, coming out of Antarctica. It keeps the water around 50 degrees year-round and prevents it from raining. There are places to the south of Lima in the Atacama Desert that have experienced no rainfall since the 1500s. It is a beautiful place, but the only green is where people are allowed to water their yards and the local parks.

One morning in Lima, I was standing on an imposing stairway with red carpet, leading from the front door of the church lobby—about 30 feet down. I was watching people walk by, and I saw the captain of the ushers, whom I knew fairly well. As he walked by, right before my eyes, his face morphed into the face of a pastor I knew well in Mexico. That was something I had never experienced before, and it represented a new and different anointing for both of us. An anointing, in this case, is a special endowment by God to do a certain task. When I saw his face change, I was a bit startled, and I said, *"God, what does that mean?"* He said, *"What do you think about when you think about the person who you saw when his face changed?"* I said, *"That man in Mexico has one of the strongest gifts of administration I have ever seen. He has the ability to organize and motivate others!"* He said, *"I have anointed the captain of the ushers with the same anointing, and it is going to grow as time goes by."* Because of that experience, I was able to help him identify and use his gift.

Since then, on numerous occasions, when I least expect it, and only when God wants, I have operated in that same anointing. In a church that I started in Texas, I was serving as an interim pastor until God brought the permanent pastor. One night, a man I had never seen before walked in with his wife. When I saw him, for a split second, his face morphed into the face of a pastor I know, and God whispered in my heart the word "pastor." I walked over to him and said in Spanish, *"Good evening, pastor!"* He said, *"Where do you know me from?"* I said, *"As far as I know, I have never seen you before, but when I first saw you, God said, 'pastor.'"* His wife sat down, put her face in her hands, and began to cry. He said, *"I was a pastor before, but I'm not pastoring now. I'm in the construction business."* I told him that I was glad to meet him. He and his wife became faithful members of the church, and as the years passed and the traveling ministry started taking me away, he became the associate pastor and cared for the church in my absence. When the ministry eventually moved me to the next place, he took the church, and at the time of this writing, he and his wife are doing very well.

22

DIVINE ENCOUNTER IN TRUJILLO

I lived on the 8th floor of a building about a half-mile from the church in Lima. It was convenient because everything was within walking distance, so I did not need a car or to pay for a taxi that cost from $2-$5 in those days.

One morning the pastor called me and asked me to come in for an appointment. I met with him, and he said, *"I am sending you and my father-in-law to Trujillo, 400 miles up the coast to the north. There is a pastor there who called, and I want for you to go and baptize his church in the Holy Spirit."* I asked him to fill me in, and he said, *"The pastor in Trujillo will fill you in when you get there."*

I had never been to Trujillo, and the terrorism made me a bit nervous. However, the pastor said that a bus was secure, and I was given a bus ticket. When we departed from the bus station in Lima, everyone had a seat, making the ride comfortable. But at what seemed like every corner, the bus stopped and took on more passengers, and before too long, people stood in the aisles and sat on armrests and every empty space. It was an interesting trip. If I looked out the window, I could see a road with barely enough room for another car to pass, and there was a sheer cliff of 200 feet leading down to rocks and the Pacific Ocean.

I was delighted when we arrived in Trujillo 10 hours later. A man met us at the bus station and drove us to the pastor's house. In those days, Trujillo was the second-largest city in Peru and had a population of around a million.

After resting a while, the pastor and his two deacons invited us into the pastor's large dining room, and I asked them to tell me what was going on in their lives. The pastor explained:

> *"Pastor Mark, we are Baptists. About a month ago, my two deacons and I were in different places, and we all began to feel dizzy, and suddenly with no warning, a strange language started coming out of our mouths. So, the two deacons each called separately and told me about their experience. They both nervously asked me what had happened, and I told them that I wasn't sure what it meant, but the same thing had happened to me. I advised them to be quiet about it and pray because we didn't want anyone to think we were crazy."*

I asked the pastor if he had ever read about his experience in the Bible, and he said he had not. Then I asked if there were any Full Gospel churches in town. They said that besides the large Catholic Church, they were the only other church to their knowledge, and they had just 30 in attendance! I also asked him how he was introduced to the pastor who sent us there to preach, and he said:

> *"Last Sunday, there was a visitor to our church. While we were worshiping the Lord, the visitor raised his hands in the air and began to sing in that strange language. I waited until after the service and asked him what that language was and where he learned it. He told me that it was tongues, and he was surprised to find out that we didn't do that because he thought all Christians did! He said that he was from Lima and gave me your pastor's telephone number. I called him, and your pastor said he would send you over here to help us. So, tell me, what can we do? If that is from God, I want all my people to have it offered to them, but what is its function, and how does it work?"*

I got out the Bible, and for about 30 minutes, I showed them 1 Corinthians 12 and 14 and explained the purpose of the gift of tongues and our prayer language. I explained that it was for power-evangelism, and if Trujillo had a population of a million, they needed a large church to train people to win the city for Jesus.

He told us that we had three days to minister to his church. Then, for the last service, he wanted us to give an invitation for people to receive the Holy Spirit with the evidence of speaking in other tongues.

We preached twice a day for two days, and at the last meeting, I said:

> *"We are going to give you an opportunity to receive the Holy Spirit and speak in tongues. So, everyone that wants to receive the Holy Spirit, come up to the front, and everyone who doesn't want Him, please stay in your seats."*

There were about 15 women and 15 men present, and all the ladies, except the pastor's wife, came to the front. All the men stayed in their seats with their arms folded, with negative expressions on their faces. The pastor's wife was nice, but she refused to come up.

I said, *"That's OK! We'll work with what we have!"* I asked everyone to repeat the prayer to receive the Holy Spirit, and halfway through the prayer, the men, who had all refused to come forward, began to cry and tremble and shake, and some slid down out of their chairs to the floor, and others just sat there and shook. One by one, they started shouting in other tongues! When the women saw what was going on, they received *en masse* and began to pray loudly in tongues, all before I could finish the prayer. The man who had come from Lima to help me preach asked me what we were supposed to do, and I said, *"Let's just go over to the side and watch because we have nothing to do with this!"*

The pastor's wife suddenly jumped to her feet and looked behind her with a startled look. Every time she tried to sit down, her waist jerked forward. Finally, she went to the altar and nervously raised her hands in the air. The next thing I knew, she hit the floor and slithered around like a snake; after less than a minute, she started jumping up and down, shouting, *"I'm free! I'm free!"* We watched for almost an hour as the Lord Jesus Himself baptized that church in the Holy Ghost.

After the service, I asked the pastor's wife what happened to her, and she said something pushed her off her seat. She said:

> *"I was thinking, 'I'm a good Baptist, and we don't do this!' So I tried to sit down, and every time I did, I felt two hands on the seat of my pants pushing me forward, so I decided that I had better go forward, and you saw the rest."*

Today, Trujillo has a vibrant, Holy Ghost church where God's Spirit is free to move, and the people there are given the opportunity to receive Jesus as their Savior.

23

TERRORISM & BOMBINGS

True terrorism is a frightful thing. When I lived in Lima during the times of the Shining Path terrorist group, we could set our clocks by the bombings every morning. At 6 AM on the dot, a car bomb would go off in a different part of the city. For all anyone knew, your street was next, and one of those cars parked out there could be packed with explosives! The result is that no one can sleep, so it causes public exhaustion. It is called terrorism for a good reason.

When we first arrived in Lima, we were asked to go by the U.S. Embassy to copy our passports and record our address and telephone number so they could find us in an emergency. Because of all of these happenings, I walked around for a year with a cloud of fear over my head.

On August 17, 1992, I was teaching in the Bible College at church, and suddenly everyone's ears popped. The windows blew open with a crash but did not break; they were forced open by the shock wave. Then, someone screamed, *"A bomb went off! Do you think we should leave?"* I learned in the forest during my encounter with the spirit of the Black Hole that running is not a good approach, so I told them that we would stay. Five minutes later, a policeman entered and said, *"We have found another bomb at the gas station on the corner, and if it goes off, it will take out the block. We are asking everyone to evacuate, but go to the left out of the door because the bomb is at the corner on the right."*

We went to the left in an orderly fashion, and I could see the 9-story building where we lived about a quarter of a mile away, and it had no glass in it. My sixteen-year-old-son was there, and I was concerned about him, so I ran home. Along the way, there were dead bodies in different places, and the police were directing people to keep moving. Finally, I got to our building and ran up the stairs because there was a power blackout. Jason was there with a cut on his face in the middle of a lot of broken glass, and he was pretty shaken up. Thankfully, we were physically okay but terrorized.

The U.S. Embassy contacted us and said:

> *"We are evacuating all U.S. Citizens because the situation here has become so unstable that we cannot guarantee your safety. We are getting some flights together, so get what you can carry in a suitcase, and we will take you to the airport."*

I asked my son if he wanted to go, and he said that he did not. I told the person on the telephone, *"We will go if we can take 10,000 Christians with us."* She said, *"Only U.S. Citizens."* I refused their kind offer. They warned me that they would not offer us help if we were captured and emphasized this was our last chance. I replied, *"God didn't tell me that I was going to die here, so I will be okay."* She hung up, and that was the last we heard from them.

After that, the fear was so bad that it seemed like everyone we saw was a terrorist, and every car seemed to be packed with explosives. I did not want to walk in fear, but I could not help it. I was jumpy. If a car backfired, I would jump! It was difficult.

On the way to church one day, I walked past a car on the street, and the devil said, *"What if that's a car bomb?"* I thought about it for a minute, and I realized I was just so tired of it all. I had not been sleeping well. The water was off, and bathing was hard, if not impossible. There was electricity for only eight hours per day, and everyone was scared. I guess you could say I had enough! I stopped, and I said out loud:

> *"Devil, if that's a car bomb, you blow me up right now in the Name of Jesus because I will go straight to heaven as a martyr, and according to the Law of Sowing and Reaping, you will reap 100 missionaries over here that are 100 times more anointed than I am! Go ahead! If that's a car bomb, blow me up right now!"*

The devil confused me for a second when he said, *"Watch your confession!"* I had to think about it for a second, but then I said:

> *"Devil, that IS my confession! If you kill me, you will succeed in destroying yourself like you did when you killed Jesus, but on a much smaller scale! Do it! I dare you! I will be on my way to heaven, and you will be finished in this country."*

With all the bombings and fear, nobody paid any attention to me out on the street arguing with an invisible foe, but I stood there for a few minutes, and I said, *"Yeah! I thought so! You coward! You wouldn't dare!"*

Something happened when I walked away from that car; the fear was gone! I walked down the road rejoicing. God had given me victory over that fear that I lived in day-to-day for the rest of my time in Peru!

Later that night, I was praying in tongues, and I am not sure if I was dreaming or if it was a vision, but this is what I saw:

I was standing on a hill in a beautiful place. I felt completely at home, which I had not felt in years. I could see mountains and forests, and there was a nighttime sky in broad daylight, and the stars were brilliant, like jewels hanging in the sky. The light was not like it is here but was yellow-colored. I looked down at my feet, and I was barefooted, standing in the grass. I could see the sand it was growing in, and I leaned down and took it between my fingers, and each grain was made of a substance that looked like solid gold. I looked over to the left, and I could see houses, but it was not like they had been built; it was like they grew there, and there were flags of jubilee flying from them.

I immediately snapped out of it, and I heard the words: *"The martyr's reward."*

A couple of years later, I heard the testimony of an elderly lady who had gone to heaven, and she told of the nighttime sky in broad daylight and the yellow light of heaven. She said that the sky is like that because the light is not the light of a star, and although it is much more brilliant than the natural world, it is like being in a large city at night. There is light from streetlights, but the sky is dark. The light there is the light of the glory of God, so it is not the prism-colored light from the sun but has a brilliant yellow hue.

Shortly thereafter, I was praying for the United States. I wore clothes bought in the United States; I was born in Texas, and my Bible was printed in Miami! I paid the bills and tithed with U.S. dollars supplied by some kind people from churches in the United States! The blood of missionaries born in the United States was on the ground here. I had seen so many incredible miracles as God poured out His Holy Spirit on Peru, but at the same time, the United States seemed to be getting worse and worse!

It was late on a Saturday night, and I could not sleep. I felt as if my heart was broken. I prayed, *"God, how could You? Here we are over here doing Your will, and it seems to me like You are letting the United States go down the drain! When will we see this happen there?"*

I was lying on the floor, and then in a vision, I saw South America, and it was in flames. I said, *"God is Peru to burn?"* Then out of the fire, an army came marching two by two toward the north. The people were bloody, had ashes and soot on their faces, and some of their clothes were tattered and torn. I said, *"God, what is that?"* He said, *"That is My great army, marching north for the conquest of the United States."* Then suddenly I was standing on a platform in a huge place. I felt the pressure of the presence of God and was afraid, so I peeked out of the corner of my eyes to the right, and I saw the foot of a large chair and someone sitting on it. He said, *"Son of man, this is heaven, and you will witness the armies of the Earth coming home after the conquest of the Earth."* I heard the marching of feet, and there was a massive parade deck in front of us. In the military, a parade deck is where an army marches in front of commanding officers or dignitaries.

In front of the armies, there was the humble Man of Galilee, leading His troops home; He was followed by one country after another. I saw African countries, European countries, Asian countries, Arabs, and Latin American nations, each carrying his flag, marching past us, giving an "eyes left," as the troops looked at us. After what seemed like a long time, I said, *"Oh Lord! Where is the United States! I didn't see them!"* After I said that, a massive army appeared on the horizon, and I saw the American flag, followed by an army of people larger than any of the others. It was made up of people of all colors and descriptions, and they were battle-hardened and dirty, but they were home! As they walked by, the voice of the Lord said,

> *"Son of man, I am not unrighteous to forget the United States. Because of them, the rest of these are here but remember the last shall be first, and the first shall be last. The United States is a country among many, and you must wait for the missionaries."*

The next day was Sunday, and I was still thinking about my experience as I went to church. After the worship service, a Peruvian man got up to prophesy. He said:

> *"Thus says the Lord, 'Pray for the United States. Because of them, you are enjoying this time of salvation. The sign of My coming will be when this outpouring of the Holy Spirit that we enjoy goes to the land of the missionaries.'"*

That cinched it for me. God will win the United States, but He will do it as He has done for centuries: through missionaries. So, welcome that stranger into your midst because they are coming!

24

IS THE MISSIONARY LIFE WORTH IT?

Betrayal is a horrible thing. It is such a part of the human experience that the Lord Jesus Himself picked someone to be a disciple that He already knew would betray Him. It is crucial to understand betrayal because if we are going to walk with Christ throughout a lifetime of faithful service, we will suffer as He did. We might expect an enemy to betray us, but unfortunately, for it to be true betrayal, it must come from a friend.

After giving much thought and prayer to the subject of betrayal, I have concluded that for Jesus to be our substitute, He had to suffer everything that we suffer. Jesus chose Judas so that his betrayal would cause that very suffering to be the undoing of the devil, who is the source of our suffering! The devil "anointed" Judas to destroy Jesus, but that act of destruction is precisely what fulfilled our destiny. Satan's undoing and ultimate end were set in motion when he moved Judas to betray Jesus. Adam betrayed God and, by so doing, brought sin and death on us all. When Jesus suffered betrayal and the resulting death in our place, He set us free from the sin and death that we inherited from Adam.

I will not speak of the events surrounding betrayals in my life, but I will talk about the One who stood with me during that time.

> Blessed is the man that endureth temptation: for when he is tried, he shall receive the crown of life, which the Lord hath promised to them that love him (James 1:12).

In this verse, many versions of the Bible translate the word "temptation" as *trial.* In every trial or battle, there is a lesson. When we overcome an attack for our faith in Christ, we receive a crown. A crown being placed on a head represents a God-given revelation. If we apply ourselves to overcoming and enduring attacks, we will be crowned with a teaching, which can be quite eye-opening.

During times of betrayal, we find out who our friends are and who is associating with us for what they can gain. If the betrayal is severe enough, it can almost reboot our identity and ministry. When the Lord Jesus was betrayed, it cost Him everything. Thank God that He was betrayed as our substitute and because He overcame, so can we. Betrayal can benefit us if we take it like soldiers and stay at our posts.

I can endure personal attacks, knowing that they eventually end. Still, one attack was particularly heinous because it came from a friend and was directed against the ministry. The attack and its repercussions lasted more than three years, and it was so severe that due to necessity, I spent 22 months on the road preaching without going home.

> In weariness and painfulness, in watchings often, in hunger and thirst, in fastings often, in cold and nakedness. Beside those things that are without, that which cometh upon me daily, the care of all the churches. Who is weak, and I am not weak? who is offended, and I burn not?... I will come to visions and revelations of the Lord (2 Corinthians 11:27-29, 12:1).

After 15 months of tribulation, I preached at a church in a rural area. While there, I lay awake a good part of the night, reflecting on the problems and rewards of missionary life. Was it all worth it? When I finally fell asleep, I had a vivid dream:

I was in a large place, almost like a stadium, with a large group of people milling around. Some were carrying boxes, and others were busily completing tasks; still, many were watching and helping the ones that were working. I looked to my left, and a large angel was standing next to me. He pointed to a group of people and said, *"That group is the long-term missionaries. Those next to them are short-term missionaries, and that other group are the givers. Every group circulates around and supports the long-term missionaries."*

I was observing the entire thing, and in the dream, I could still feel the pain of betrayal and the questions in my heart. Then, suddenly across the room from me, a large, brown-skinned man stepped out in the open. He appeared to be in charge as all eyes were on him. The tan slacks he wore accented his 32-inch waist, and a light tan tee-shirt defined his broad shoulders and huge biceps. His neatly combed light brown hair was cut in a short businessman's haircut, and he was clean-shaven.

The angel continued to talk, but I did not hear him because my attention was drawn to the large man. I interrupted him and asked, *"Pardon, me! Who's the big guy?"* The angel said, *"He's the head missionary."* I said, *"Oh? What's his name?"* The angel responded quite naturally, *"Why, He's the Lord Jesus Christ."* I was shocked! My mouth dropped open, and I felt my heart come up in my throat, and the tears began to flow. I managed to say to the angel, *"Excuse me, sir, but I can't help it! I've always wanted to do this!"* I have heard of people who were afraid in encounters with God, but I did not care. My pain had been exquisite, and all I wanted to do was get close to Him! I ran as fast I could, and when I came up to Him, I began to weep almost uncontrollably. I said, *"Oh, Lord Jesus! I am so grateful to You! You saved my soul from hell! You have done so many things for me."*

In the dream, I was sobbing so deeply that I felt like I was drowning in tears, and all I could say was, *"Thank You! Thank You!"* He looked at me, and through my tears, I saw Him pull off His tee-shirt. He showed me His muscles, and He was perfect; I felt so small in His presence. Looking me square in the eyes, He shouted with a booming voice of authority and power, *"You've got Me, Mark!"* I said, *"Oh! I just can't stand it!"* While still crying, I walked up to Him and stood on my toes and kissed Him on His left cheek. In His acceptance and compassion, He put his left arm around me and pulled me close and said quietly in my ear, *"It's OK; it's OK."* What does all of this mean?

The apostle Paul ended his talk in 2 Corinthians chapter 11 by starting the next chapter by saying, "I will come to visions and revelations of the Lord" (2 Corinthians 12:1b). It seems as if Paul implies that visions and revelations of the Lord follow persecution.

So, **why is the missionary life worth it?** What is the meaning of all our tribulation and the teaching hidden in our battles? Jesus is our reward; He is the recompense. Prosperity and worldly wealth are wonderful things, but the greatest "thing" we can receive is Jesus Himself. He is our recompense and reward.

> Yea doubtless, and I count all things but loss for the excellency of the knowledge of Christ Jesus my Lord: for whom I have suffered the loss of all things, and do count them but dung, that I may win Christ (Philippians 3:8).

25

UNCLE WALLACE'S APPOINTMENTS

Noted Christian author, C. S. Lewis stated, "There are only two kinds of people in the end: those who say to God, 'Thy will be done,' and those to whom God says in the end, 'Thy will be done.'"[5]

Life is a mystery. It is a combination of events that grow together into a picture intended to communicate God's ability to take something undone and make a beautiful picture out of it.

We are that picture, and the coordination of events that makes up our lives is what we call "our testimony." As we get older and people pass away, we arrive at a place in life where all we have left is our testimony, and it is the very thing that we take with us to heaven! It is our treasure that "moth and rust cannot corrupt and that thieves cannot break through to steal." It is the substance of our lives spent serving the Master.

My Cherokee Indian Great Uncle was in the ministry from the 1930s until his death in 1992. I got to know him after I turned 19, and he taught me many things about the Holy Spirit and ministry.

Uncle Wallace was an incredible man, and the anointing was strong with him. He told me one particular story about his life that significantly impacted me:

Many years ago, my uncle was doing a cabinetry job in Houston. One day he was cutting through a board with his circular saw, and the Lord Jesus came to him and said through the Holy Spirit, *"Go to Fouke, Arkansas."* He tried to explain to the Lord that he was in the middle of a job and this kitchen was a mess, so he committed to go when he was finished. However, the Lord kept pressing him about it, so he asked the Lord, *"Would You please speak to the woman about it? I can't be a bad businessman. I will ask, and if she approves, I will go, but I cannot leave her with this mess without her approval!"* He called to the lady of the house and said, *"I'm so sorry, but the Lord Jesus keeps telling me that He wants me to go to Arkansas. However, I don't want to go until I'm finished because your kitchen is such a mess!"* To his surprise, the lady said, *"No! If the Lord Jesus is telling you to do something, you do it right now! You must obey Him. The kitchen will be here when you get back."*

Uncle Wallace only had enough money for a week in Fouke if he stayed in an inexpensive hotel. So, he left the next day and drove approximately 300 miles. Finding a room, he went into prayer, fully expecting something supernatural to happen. He spent an uneventful week praying, and the last evening, he said, *"Lord, I have to leave. I don't have any more money. If you want me to do something special here, please tell me what it is."* Other than spending a week in prayer, nothing happened, and he went back to Houston.

Uncle Wallace's story continued:

> *"I didn't know what was going on. Had I missed God? Why would He send me that far to sit and pray in a hotel room for a week? However, the night I got back to Houston, I had a vivid dream where I was sitting in front of a small round table with a jigsaw puzzle on it. I could see that parts of it fit together, but most of it was scattered all over the tabletop, and it was unclear what the finished product would be. As I pondered what the puzzle would be when it was all put together and what it meant, suddenly I could feel someone standing behind me. He was wearing a white robe and reached over my right shoulder, and when He did, I could clearly see His Hand and the hole from the nail. Then, He reached down, took a piece of the puzzle, carefully fit it to another piece, and said, '**Son, this was your trip to Arkansas.**'"*

We cannot control what happens to us in life, but we can walk with Jesus, expecting to hear His voice through it all. He speaks, again and again, but do we hear? Job 33:14 says, "For God speaketh once, yea twice, yet man perceiveth it not."

When my uncle was 80, I visited him in Kansas City, Missouri, just before he passed away. I asked him how he was doing, and he said they told him he had liver cancer, and there was no cure. So, I said:

> *"Let me pray for you like you did for me when I was crippled from that car wreck. When God heals you, you can travel with me and tell your testimony. Then, once you are ready, you can pass away from something else."*

I was surprised at his response:

> *"I know God will heal me if I ask Him to, but I have lived my life. I do not want to go back to the pulpit; I am ready to go to heaven. Let me tell you what happened to me in a Kansas snowstorm five years ago. I got caught in a blizzard and could not see. I thought I could make it to the house and decided to walk, but I couldn't find my way. I was wearing only a sweater, and it was five degrees with a hard-north wind and blowing snow. I was so cold and tired, so I sat down and tried to keep warm by folding my arms, closing my eyes, and doubling up. I literally 'chilled out.' After a while, I wasn't cold anymore, so I looked up, and I was on my feet, standing on something and flying along. I saw the stars, but they weren't going past me; I was speeding along, going past them, one by one.*

> *It wasn't a vision because I felt normal. I looked off in the distance and saw a light getting bigger and bigger as I headed toward it. All at once, I realized that I had died! I thought about seeing mom and daddy, all the old folks, and the Lord Jesus, and I was so happy. I laid my head back and shouted, 'YEE-HA!' And do you know what happened? I shouted myself back into my body again. I woke up, and someone was reviving me! I just want to let you know, Mark, this time when it happens, I'm going to keep my mouth shut!"*

I could see that he was determined to leave, so I asked him to do like Jacob did in the Bible—pray for me and prophesy over my life, which he did.

[5]C. S. Lewis, The Great Divorce (New York City: HarperCollins, 1946), 75.

26

TO KNOW HIM

"But the path of the just is as the shining light, that shineth more and more unto the perfect day" (Proverbs 4:18).

After all these years, it never ceases to amaze me when I consider how my eyes open more and more to perceive the truths that are revealed in this life. I want to know Him! As a young man, I was a bit more sure of myself, and if God had left me in that condition, I suppose my growth would have been stunted. However, He has kept His hand on me all along, and His Word to me has always been what Jesus said in Mark 1:38, "Let us go into the next towns, that I may preach there also: for therefore came I forth."

Proverbs talks about "...the path of the just ... that shineth more and more..." (Proverbs 4:18). To be on a path that gets brighter and brighter, we must be going someplace. Jesus has kept me on the move throughout my life and has challenged me to continue "ever onward" on my path of discovery toward the stars. The highway and its challenges have made me unsure of myself because I know that what He wants of me is far beyond me and my capabilities. I have found that I need Him. If we are true disciples, Jesus will give us a custom-designed plan for our lives that will cause us to grow into His stature!

I have become aware of the Christian circle of life, and 1 John 2:13 illustrates this. First, it says, "I **write** unto you fathers because you have known him who is from the beginning" (1 John 2:13). Then, in the next verse, John says again, "I **have written** unto you, fathers, because ye have known him that is from the beginning" (1 John 2:14). This repetition and the change in the verb tense show us that very circle and how we begin at the altar and end up at the same place.

When my Christian life began at that altar in 1963, all I could say was, *"Jesus Christ, Son of God, have mercy on me: a sinner."* Years later, when I seriously began to "get right with God," I believed that I was getting it all together as I confessed the Scripture, *"I am the righteousness of God in Christ. I am the head and not the tail. I am blessed. I am…I am…I am…."* But now, although my confession of faith has not changed, I find myself back at that same altar of 1963, looking at Jesus Christ and saying once again, *"Son of God, have mercy on me: a sinner."* It does not matter how much I seem to know or what I have accomplished; the road and the next place always press me higher to another level, where my experience and efforts are not enough to succeed.

As a disciple of Jesus of Nazareth, I have learned that there is a **secret to success in life**, and it is not a formula or blueprint. The secret to success is Jesus Himself and what only He personally can supply. To be successful, we must have His presence and be obedient to His customized plan for our lives, no matter where we go, what we do, or the circumstances we find in the world around us when we get there.

Life with Jesus brings us to the sweet awakening of the new day and the next place. We spend our lives studying the Scripture, but the Bible with no corresponding action only leaves us with itching ears. We may have success as far as worldly things are concerned, but without radical action on our part, we may never amount to much in Christ. The day is soon coming in everyone's life in which, like it or not, success in the spiritual realm is all that **will** matter. We remember that Hebrews 11:6 says, "But without faith it is impossible to please [God]." The simplest way to define "faith" is to say that true faith is just doing what the Bible says. If we fail to **do** the Bible, it shows we do not believe it. Likewise, we may never see His Hand at work in a personal way if we fail to attempt the supernatural based on that Bible!

To have faith, we must do something! The experience of discipleship has taught that Christian maturity is not and never will be what we "have" or what we "have done;" it will never be that we reach a place of having it all together or of sinless perfection. On the contrary, that maturity is shown as we quietly and reverently reach a point in our trials where we stop looking at ourselves. Like the great apostle, we learn that looking at ourselves truthfully and with older eyes will always cause a Romans 7 "woe is me" sense of hopelessness and despair. So, we look at Him, strive to know Him, and discover that our true reward is not heaven and paradise, but He Himself and being close to Him. He belongs to us, and we finally comprehend that we belong to Him. We see once and for all that we are His responsibility, and He Who began that good work in us so long ago will most certainly finish it. So, I re-join my 7-year-old self, kneeling in tears at that altar, and I say with fear and trembling, *"Jesus Christ, Son of God, have mercy on me!"*

Let's go! Which way do we go? "Second star to the right and straight on 'til morning!"[6]

[6]J. M. Barrie, Peter and Wendy (1911) In the Public Domain.

ABOUT THE AUTHOR

MARK SCRIVENER is driven by the heart of a pastor and the fire of an evangelist. The apostolic anointing on his life and supernatural insight have allowed God to use him in various positions of ministry including pastor, teacher, and missionary. His fluency in Spanish and compassion for the Spanish-speaking world have taken him throughout the Americas, building and restoring God's Kingdom. Dr. Scrivener often serves as an adjunct professor at several Bible colleges; he holds a Doctorate in Ministry for Missions. He currently resides with his wife, Alma, in the great state of Texas.

For more information, contact:

mark@scrivenerministries.org • markjs2015@gmail.com
www.scrivenerministries.org • 832-523-9258